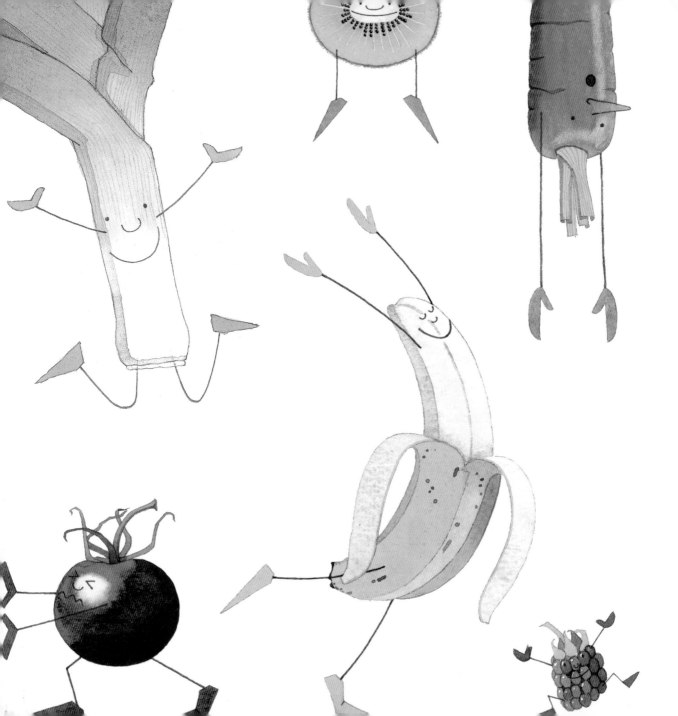

Annabel Karmel's
Baby-Led
Weaning
Recipe
Book

120 Recipes to Let Your Baby Take the Lead

St. Martin's Griffin
New York

CONTENTS

INTRODUCTION

For over 25 years, my delicious, nutritious baby and toddler recipes have graced the tables (and quite probably the walls and floors) of millions of households worldwide. Tales of proud weaning conquests regularly flood my inbox, and I take great pleasure in seeing photos and videos of babies demolishing my recipes.

So what's my recipe for success in getting so many babies and children to eat well? My mantra is simple: experiment with a wide variety of healthy foods, flavors, and textures early on in a baby's weaning journey.

Lots of parents find themselves feeling apprehensive about weaning and that's only natural. After all, you've finally found your comfort zone with breastfeeding and formula! You ask yourself, what foods should I start with? How much should they be having? Should I be trying baby-led weaning, and what if they choke?

While many parents start out with smooth purees for spoon feeding, baby-led weaning (BLW) is quickly growing in popularity. Some feel a need to go with one method or the other, but you don't have to choose. At around six months, you have the freedom to combine an element of baby-led weaning along with spoon feeding if you feel that's right for you and your baby. The key is to go at your baby's pace and give her the opportunity to explore lots of different tastes and textures. Combining purees and soft finger foods at the beginning is appealing to many families.

And that's why I've devised my *Baby-Led Weaning Recipe Book*—to be used on its own for those wanting to explore BLW, or to be used as a companion cookbook to my bestselling *Top 100 Baby Purees*, which contains my favorite puree recipes.

Whichever approach you adopt, I'll be there to support you and your baby along the way with delicious, nutritious recipes, simple methods, and clear advice for giving your child the very best start.

What is BLW and how is it different from feeding purees?

There are two ways of weaning: spoon-feeding purees and BLW. Moms know me for my failsafe puree recipes, starting out with smooth textures and simple flavors, then introducing new tastes and textures, and soft, cooked finger foods around six months, or as soon as your baby is able to pick up food and bring it to her mouth.

The philosophy behind BLW is to let your baby feed herself from six months' old, omitting purees and spoon feeding. It gives babies the opportunity to explore a variety of different tastes and textures from the beginning, helping them to eat a wide range of food, and develop good eating habits from the start.

Signs that your baby is ready to feed themselves

Look out for these signs that indicate your baby is ready to start feeding herself soft chunks and textures:

* She can sit up unassisted.
* She has lost the tongue-thrust reflex (automatically pushing solids out of her mouth with her tongue).
* She has developed sufficient hand-eye coordination to pick up food and put it in her mouth.
* She is able to chew, even if she has few or no teeth.
* She shows that she wants to join in family mealtimes.

At first, your baby may just play with the food you give them, but this is all part of their development. They will soon progress to sucking, chewing, and swallowing.

Premature babies are advised to begin weaning earlier than the recommended 26 weeks, so are not suitable for BLW from the beginning. They often have delays in their development, which mean that, by six months, they may not be able to sit up unassisted or be able to pick up and interact with food.

Milk feeds

It is important to remember when starting your baby on solids that milk is still the best and most natural food for growing babies and it contains all the nutrients your baby needs for the first six months. Breastmilk is best and if there is a history of allergy in the family it is particularly important to try and breastfeed exclusively for six months before introducing solids. Babies should be given breast or formula milk for the whole of the first year. Between six months and a year babies need 30–32 ounces (800–900 ml) of breastmilk or formula each day.

What are the advantages of BLW?

BLW encourages shared and social eating, with your baby enjoying family meals from the beginning of her food journey. While busy family schedules don't always allow time for eating together, it's a positive principle to adopt, even if it's only a few times a week.

Regularly offering a variety of family meals (without added salt or sugar) encourages babies to adopt good eating habits, because these foods, which often offer a wider variety of tastes and textures than a spoon-fed diet, become a regular part of their diet. Babies that are only offered a limited variety of foods could develop fussiness, whereas babies and young children that are given foods such as curry and chili con carne tend to accept new foods more willingly. Also, spices add flavor to food without the need for salt.

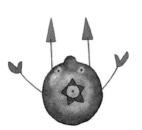

What are the advantages of spoon-fed purees?

While the American Academy of Pediatrics (AAP) recommends that babies should not begin weaning before six months and should be exclusively breastfed for the first six months, babies do develop at their own pace. If your baby is showing signs of being ready to move on from breastfeeding or formula milk, you can try giving simple solids from 17 weeks, but not before, as your baby's digestive system will not be sufficiently developed to cope with food other than breast or formula milk.

Before six months, babies tend not to have developed the hand-eye coordination which is essential in BLW and therefore it should not be attempted. Purees or well-mashed food are an obvious bridge between liquid and solid foods and it's easy for you to see how much your baby is eating if you spoon-feed her.

When your baby reaches six months, the World Health Organization and U.S. National Library of Medicine recommends giving your baby iron-rich pureed meats, fruits, and vegetables at the beginning of weaning, as well as soft finger foods.

From six months, your baby starts to need iron from food, as breastmilk alone won't give him enough. If your baby is just starting out weaning at six months, giving iron-rich foods such as chicken or meat without some form of pureeing or mashing can make it difficult for babies to eat, which could mean they are missing out on essential nutrients. Some young babies also don't cope as well as others with lumpy food and need a more gradual transition from milk to solids.

A flexible approach to weaning

I believe there is a third way to weaning which involves giving purees when a baby is ready for first foods (particularly if slightly earlier than six months), with the introduction of finger foods and family meals from around six months.

Official advice advocates giving a mix of purees and soft finger foods in the beginning, and in speaking to parents, dietitians, and healthcare professionals about weaning, this flexible approach is now the preferred option, and one that many are finding the most realistic to adopt.

What's important is that there is no right or wrong to weaning. It's about what works for you and your family. The key is to go at your baby's pace and give her the opportunity to explore lots of different tastes and textures. Combining purees and finger foods is, for many families, a good compromise.

With this flexible approach in mind, my *Baby-Led Weaning Recipe Book* has been designed as the ultimate companion book to my classic *Top 100 Baby Purees*. It uses everyday mealtime ingredients that your baby can feed themselves, and paired with my Meal Planner (which starts out with purees), it will help you and your baby get the very best out of both weaning methods.

As with BLW, purees can also fit into the family routine. If you are preparing a fish pie or lasagne for the family, simply skip the added salt and blend your baby's portion to the desired texture.

And, whether you choose spoon-feeding, BLW, or a mix of both, it's important to realize that your baby will instinctively tell you whether they like something or not, whether they are hungry or full, or whether they are ready to move onto something new. However you want to feed them, they will take the lead.

Registered dietician and consultant nutritionist Sarah Almond Bushell says: "My advice would be to give your baby well-mashed or pureed foods at the beginning of weaning, as well as offering finger foods which dissolve easily in the mouth. As a trusted expert in feeding, Annabel's new baby-led weaning recipes are a great addition to her puree recipes. Parents often feel pressured to try baby-led weaning, but actually it's probably better to combine the two, that way you ensure optimum nutrition while helping your baby to develop the important motor skills as well as being included in sociable family mealtimes."

How to get your baby started with self-feeding

* Make sure you have a safe place for your baby to sit. A highchair is the best option. Your baby should be able to sit upright unassisted. Then you need appropriate finger foods. The key is to take your baby's lead and feed them solids once a day to start with, gradually increasing quantities as she shows she wants more.
* Make mealtimes a fun experience. Even if eating together at the same time doesn't work for your family, perhaps sit down and eat a snack with her while she eats so that mealtimes don't become an isolating experience.
* Baby's first finger foods at six months should be soft and easy to swallow: fresh fruits; soft, cooked vegetables; healthy carbohydrates; and fats. Your role as the parent is to provide a variety of healthy foods that, in combination, provide a good balance of nutrients.

Safety

However your baby is fed, they should never be left alone while eating, and they must always be supported in an upright position.

It's understandable to worry about your baby choking. It's important to note that a baby who is struggling to get food into her mouth probably isn't quite ready to eat, so take your baby's lead. Whether you are feeding purees or finger foods (or both), your baby's own developmental abilities will make sure that the transition to solid foods takes place at the right time for her, reducing the risk of choking. That's why it's important to start weaning only when your baby shows signs she is ready.

It's also important to differentiate between gagging and choking. Gagging is a safety mechanism that prevents choking by pushing food away from the airway if the food is too big to be swallowed. The gag reflex in babies is triggered toward the front of the tongue (unlike adults where it is farther back). That's why finger foods are recommended from six months, as your baby learns to chew and swallow when this reflex is safely close to the front of the mouth.

Choking occurs when the airway is completely or partially blocked. A baby who is choking is usually silent rather than coughing and spluttering, as no air is getting past the blockage. In this rare instance, your baby will need help in dislodging the lump using standard First Aid measures. If her airway is only partially blocked, your baby will usually cough to clear the blockage.

It is important to note that babies can store food in their mouth for quite some time after eating, so check that your baby has swallowed her food.

Avoid these foods that could cause choking

* Whole grapes*
* Whole cherry tomatoes*
* Whole or chopped nuts
* Fruit with pits such as cherries and lychees
* Bony fish (make sure you check for bones)

*Small round fruit should be cut up.

How much food should I give?

Feeding purees as well as solids takes some of the anxiety out of knowing whether your child is getting enough to eat.

Breastmilk (or formula) should provide all of your baby's nutritional needs for the first six months. After that, milk alone will not provide all or your baby's needs. It is important to include iron-rich foods such as meat and chicken because babies are born with an iron store that starts to run out at around six months, and a shortfall of iron is the most common nutritional deficiency in young children.

The benefit of offering purees in addition to finger foods is that it allows you to take some control, particularly if you are not sure your baby is meeting her nutritional needs through BLW alone.

Gradually increase the quantity of food you give your baby, and offer whole-fat rather than low-fat dairy foods (low in added sugar), because these are a better source of vitamin A and provide extra calories babies need for growth and development.

Cooking oils

*Unsaturated fats are the best fats to cook with for babies and adults alike and occur naturally in plant foods such as nuts, seeds, and vegetables. They can either be polyunsaturated (sunflower, soy, corn, and sesame oils) or monounsaturated (canola or olive oils). Monounsaturated oils have the benefit of being good for heart heath as they have the ability to produce HDL cholesterol (high-density lipoprotein, the "good" cholesterol). Try to avoid cooking with products that contain high levels of saturated fat, such as coconut oil, palm oil, butter, ghee, lard and suet, which can increase the risk of heart disease.

*Coconut oil has gained popularity in recent years, but there's not enough evidence as yet to suggest that coconut oil is anything other than detrimental to heart health.

*Omega-3 oils found in oily fish are great, too. Natural sources found in oily fish are the most bioavailable for a baby's growth and brain development.

Salt

Don't season your baby's food with salt before the age of one. Salt is present in some foods, such as bread, breakfast cereal, and cheese, which can be added to your baby's diet from six months and give them all the sodium their body needs.

Do check the labels of store-bought sauces and instant meals for salt content before serving them to your baby. Bouillon cubes and stock powders can also be very salty and are best avoided. Instead, make your own broth, or choose a low-salt variety (dilute it well) or an unsalted variety.

Up to the age of one, babies should consume less than 400 mg of sodium a day. From 1–3 years of age, the maximum daily intake is 800 mg sodium, and from four–six years of age, children should not consume more than 1200 mg a day.

Dairy and eggs

Whole cow's milk can be used in cooking from six months on.

Feed your child whole-fat dairy products (yogurt, cheese, etc.) for the first two years to help fuel his rapid growth.

Babies can eat whole cooked eggs, including the yolk, from six months. Due to the perceived risk of allergies, it was once recommended to give only egg yolks to babies, starting from 7–10 months, however the American Academy of Pediatricians has now determined that omitting the egg white had no effect in preventing allergies.

Fiber

Babies shouldn't have too much insoluble fiber (such as bran and whole-wheat foods) in their diet as this can deplete their bodies of vital nutrients such as iron and zinc, by binding to them and affecting their absorption. Soluble fiber, on the other hand, such as that found in oats, beans, lentils, and vegetables, does not bind to these nutrients. Ideally, give your baby a mixture of white and whole-wheat bread, pasta, and rice. Babies need proportionately more fat and less fiber in their diet than adults.

Sugar

There is no need to add sugar to your baby's food because it offers no nutritional benefits, unless you occasionally want to add a little to muffins or cookies to boost their flavor, or a pinch to a tomato sauce to reduce its acidity. You can sweeten food naturally using fruit and fruit purees.

Allergies

If you are introducing family meals to your baby, keep a close eye on potential allergens and limit the addition of salt and sugar, especially if using pre-made foods such as pasta sauces.

Food allergies are more common among babies and children from families with a history of allergy. This can be any type of allergy, from pollen to animal hair, and is not just associated with food. Babies who suffer from eczema are also at risk of suffering from food allergies. Babies who develop severe eczema before the age of three months are at very high risk, so you need to be especially careful when introducing new foods.

Most serious food allergies start in infancy and early childhood. They are caused by a relatively small number of different foods. Milk, soy, and egg are the most common allergies but tend to disappear during childhood.

Until recently, parents were encouraged to delay the introduction of allergenic foods such as milk, eggs, or peanuts, but in fact, there is now substantial evidence to suggest that early introduction of eggs and peanuts can reduce the risk of a child forming an allergy. In some countries, such as Israel for example, peanut is used in a snack called Bamba which is given to infants. This early weaning with a peanut product seems to relate to a corresponding low level of peanut allergy, even among children at high-risk. In 2016, doctors at St. Thomas' Hospital in London were able to show that children who ate products containing ground peanuts between the ages of four and eleven months, and regularly thereafter, had a 70% reduced risk of developing an allergy to peanuts, compared with children who ate them for the first time when they were older.

Diagnosing food allergies relies on a careful analysis of medical history, examination, and tests. The best treatment is to completely avoid the problem food. Speak to your doctor and ask for a referral to a pediatric dietitian before avoiding food groups because you do not want to cut out nutrients without replacing them with other food sources. Your doctor will ask about the symptoms of the reaction and whether they happen every time the food is eaten.

With immediate reactions, testing can be done by a blood test or by a "skin prick" test, where food extracts are placed on the skin of the arm and gently pricked. The results of either test can be very helpful in confirming if the allergy is present.

What to do if your child chokes

I encourage all new parents to become familiar with First Aid procedures for children, especially if they are concerned about choking risks when they start weaning. Visit the American Red Cross or American Heart Association websites, which offer online learning and classes, or ask your pediatrician's office about local courses.

High-risk foods to avoid for babies under 12 months

* Honey
* Mold-ripened soft cheeses
* Added salt and sugar
* Whole cow's milk (or goat milk/ sheep's milk) as a main drink. You can introduce a little into your baby's foods from six months, once she's started on solids
* Shark, swordfish, or marlin (due to high mercury levels)
* High choking-risk foods like whole grapes and whole/chopped nuts (although nut butters can be given at six months)
* Stimulants such as chocolate or sugar
* Unhealthy and processed foods such as battered foods, sugary breakfast cereals, french fries, and other foods that contain sugar
* Caffeinated drinks such as tea, coffee, hot chocolate, and cola

Giving you the confidence to find your own way

What I'm suggesting is a hybrid approach to feeding: provide your baby with a variety of nutrient-packed purees at the very beginning, along with soft finger foods and nutritious family meals that your baby can experiment with herself. It's all about finding out what works for you and your baby.

All recipes are suitable from six months unless marked otherwise. However, every baby develops at his or her own pace and it is important to start weaning only when your baby shows signs she is ready. Use your judgment or speak to a healthcare professional if you are unsure. Your baby should never be left alone when eating, and they must always be supported in an upright position.

All the recipes are suitable for the whole family and can be scaled up accordingly. You can also freeze extra portions for your baby where a recipe includes the "suitable for freezing" icon.

 Suitable for freezing

DAIRY FREE Dairy-free recipes (but other recipes can be made dairy-free by substituting a dairy-free margarine for butter. There are also lots of dairy-free alternatives to cow's milk made from soy, coconut, oat, and almond)

What parents say about using a flexible approach

'The general consensus among my mom friends is that you can do a bit of both. My daughter showed strong signs of wanting food at 5½ months, so I started her on purees, then introduced finger foods just after six months, which worked really well for her. I don't think you have to follow baby-led weaning exclusively." *KatieMarch*

"I did start out with baby-led weaning, but my son wasn't getting enough food, so I resorted to giving more milk. I felt that having the option of purees took the pressure off me, and while I know that a mix of the two methods isn't true baby-led weaning, it is working for us as he is getting the nutrients he needs, while also enjoying experimenting with finger foods." *Loubymama*

TOP TIPS FOR INTRODUCING FINGER FOODS AND FAMILY MEALS

1 Babies around six months tend to use their whole hand to pick things up. They need to be able to close their hand around the food, so avoid making the pieces too wide. Start with pieces that are big enough for your baby to hold in their fist with some sticking out. Fairly long pieces stand a better chance of being picked up. I would suggest cutting food into approximately 2 in (5 cm) batons or sticks so that half is held in a baby's hand and the other half sticks out.

2 Start with softer fingers foods such as cooked stalks of carrot, broccoli, and sweet potato, and chunks of banana, avocado, and cucumber. First tastes like steamed carrots should be cooked until soft but not too mushy so that your baby can grab it with their fist. Wait until your baby has teeth before you offer harder foods like raw carrot.

3 Let your baby pick up food with their fingers when they start baby-led weaning. Babies must learn to move foods safely around their mouths, so don't put food in their mouth. They will only pick up foods they can manage.

4 Brace yourself for a messy experience! It may be easier just to place the food straight onto their highchair tray rather than a plate. Choose an easy-clean highchair with a wide tray. Alternatively, choose a highchair without a tray and bring it level to the table.

5 Invest in a wipe-clean bib and a splash mat for the floor. Shower curtains are a great option and can be bought cheaply.

6 BLW is about making family mealtimes a social experience. While finger foods are important (particularly soft foods at the beginning), there's no reason why you can't serve them a portion of cottage pie, spaghetti Bolognese, or roast chicken. Just make sure you leave out the salt.

7 Don't worry if your baby doesn't like certain foods—it's important that they explore a wide variety of food independently. However, don't put too much on the highchair tray at one time, as this could be a little overwhelming. Just a couple of pieces of food, or a small portion of a family meal is enough.

8 It's very important to be aware of the food your baby shouldn't eat under the age of 12 months. Refer to page 16 for foods to avoid.

9 Wait until your baby is ready. She should be able to sit in a highchair unassisted and show signs she want to eat.

10 Don't rush your baby or encourage her to eat a set amount or specific food. She chooses what, how much, and how quickly to eat.

Banana

Cheese, cut into
sticks or chunks

Whole eggs
(including the yolk)

GOOD FINGER FOODS AT SIX MONTHS

Start with pieces of food that are big enough for your baby to hold in their clenched fist with
some sticking out. They need to be able to close their hand around the food, so don't make
the pieces too wide. Fairly long pieces stand a better chance of being picked up, and as
a general rule of thumb, a stick of food should be around 2 in (5 cm) long.

Dried fruit

Mango

Cooked pasta

Cooked stalks or chunks of carrot, broccoli, potato, sweet potato, butternut squash, or apple

Pieces of poultry (dark meat is best) or meat

Pieces of cooked fish

Cubes or fingers of bread, toast, and pita bread

Low-salt rice cakes

Low-salt breadsticks

Wholegrain cereal

Citrus fruit

Raw slices or chunks of soft foods such as avocado, cucumber, peaches, pears and strawberries

Breakfast

Little Monkey Oatmeal

MAKES 1–2 CHILD PORTIONS
½ cup rolled oats
1 cup milk
4 prunes, finely chopped
½ banana, peeled

Babies love bananas and they are a great first food because they are soft and bursting with nutrients. Prunes and banana make a delicious combination and the prunes help keep your baby regular.

● · ●

Put the oats, milk and chopped prunes in a small saucepan. Stir and simmer over a medium heat for 3–4 minutes until the oats have absorbed the milk and the mixture has thickened. Remove from the heat and leave to cool for a minute or two.

Mash the banana and add it to the oatmeal.

Spoon the oatmeal into 1 or two bowls and serve.

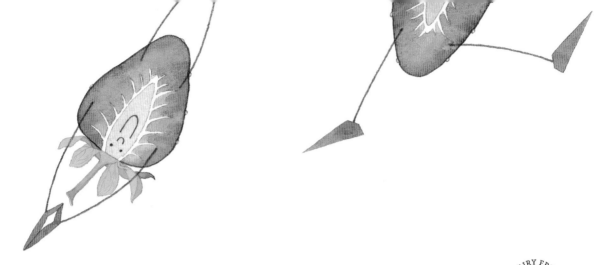

Fruit Smoothie with Oats and Almond Milk

MAKES 2 CHILD PORTIONS

1 banana

¾ cup hulled and halved fresh strawberries

1 cup fresh raspberries

⅔ cup almond milk

2 tablespoons rolled oats

¼ cup apple juice

Almond milk is very much having a "superfood" moment. It is an effective substitute for cow's milk if your toddler has a dairy allergy or intolerance. However, choose one that is fortified with calcium and vitamins. For babies under one year, you should continue with either breast milk or a specially designed infant formula which is dairy/lactose free for your baby's main drink. You could use almond milk with cereal or in cooking from six months.

• •

Place all of the ingredients in a blender and process until smooth.

For babies, serve this recipe in a sippy cup with a soft spout. You should only ever give milk or water in your baby's bottle.

My Favorite Granola

DAIRY FREE

MAKES 8 CHILD PORTIONS
2 cups rolled oats
⅔ cup finely chopped pecans
¼ cup dried unsweetened coconut
¼ teaspoon fine salt
¼ cup light soft brown sugar
2 tablespoons sunflower
    or canola oil, plus extra
    for greasing
4 tablespoons maple syrup
⅓ cup raisins

Make this and you'll never want store-bought granola again. It's super-easy to make, too. I like to serve it with plain yogurt, fresh berries, and a drizzle of maple syrup. Choose whole-milk yogurt for children under 2, to fuel their rapid growth.

• •

Preheat the oven to 300°F (150°C) and lightly grease a baking sheet with oil. Combine the oats, pecans, dried unsweetened coconut, salt, and sugar in a large bowl.

Whisk the oil and maple syrup together in a small mixing bowl, then pour the mixture over the dry ingredients and stir well to combine. Spread the granola mixture on the oiled baking sheet and bake in the middle of the oven for 40 minutes, stirring every 10 minutes. Remove from the oven, transfer to a bowl, stir in the raisins, and let cool.

Scrambled Eggs with Toppings

MAKES 2 CHILD PORTIONS

2 tablespoons butter

3 large eggs

2 tablespoons milk

a little salt and pepper (for
babies over 12 months old)

Toppings

**SCALLION, TOMATO,
AND CHEESE**

1 teaspoon light olive oil

3 scallions, sliced

1 tomato, chopped

1 tablespoon grated
Cheddar cheese

a small pinch of salt (for
babies over 12 months old)

**MUSHROOM, CHIVE,
AND CHEESE**

1 teaspoon light olive oil

1 cup sliced button mushrooms

1 teaspoon chopped chives

1 tablespoon grated
Cheddar cheese

a small pinch of salt (for
babies over 12 months old)

Eggs are a fantastic food for the whole family and are packed full of nutrients. It's fine to give whole cooked eggs to babies, including the yolk, and the great thing is that you often have them on hand so you can rustle up a quick, nutritious breakfast in a jiffy.

Melt the butter in a skillet. Beat the eggs, milk, and seasoning (if using) together in a mixing bowl, then pour it into the skillet. Stir over a medium heat until scrambled and cooked through, then remove from the heat and make your topping.

Scallion, Tomato, and Cheese Heat the oil in a skillet. Add the scallions and fry for 1 minute, then add the tomato and fry for 2 minutes more. Season with the salt (if using). Spoon the tomato and scallion mixture on top of the scrambled eggs and sprinkle with the cheese.

Mushroom, Chive, and Cheese Heat the oil in a skillet. Add the mushrooms and fry over a high heat for 3–4 minutes until golden. Season with the salt (if using). Spoon the mushrooms on top of the scrambled eggs and sprinkle with the chives and cheese.

Almond Milk Oatmeal with Berries

DAIRY FREE

MAKES 3 CHILD PORTIONS
¾ cup blueberries
1 tablespoon apple juice
⅔ cup raspberries
apple, banana, blueberries,
   and strawberries, to decorate
   (optional)

Oatmeal
½ cup rolled oats
1¼ cups almond milk
1 tablespoon maple syrup
   (optional) or use 2 tablespoons
   of apple juice

The king of all breakfasts! A bowl of oatmeal makes a great start to the day, and will give you and your baby long-lasting reserves of energy thanks to the slow release of complex carbs. Sweetening it with fresh fruit and a drizzle of maple syrup gives it extra appeal. Babies should continue with breast milk or infant formula as their main milk supply for the first year. However, you can use other milks like whole cow's milk or dairy-free options such as almond milk with cereal from six months.

• •

Put the blueberries in a small saucepan with the apple juice. Stir over a low heat for a few minutes until the blueberries are just starting to soften, then remove from the heat and add the raspberries. Set aside.

Place the oats in a small saucepan with the almond milk. Bring to a boil over a medium heat, then reduce the heat and simmer for 4–5 minutes until thickened. Add the maple syrup.

Spoon the oatmeal into bowls and top with the warm fruit.

If wished, create an owl face by topping each portion with two apple slices for wings, sliced halves of banana for feathers, wedge of strawberry for a nose, and slices of bananas topped with blueberries for eyes.

Banana, Carrot, and Seed Bread ❋

MAKES 1 LOAF
⅔ cup softened unsalted butter
2 large eggs
⅔ cup peeled and mashed ripe
   bananas
⅞ cup grated carrot
2 tablespoons golden raisins
⅝ cup soft dark brown sugar
1¾ cups self-rising flour
½ teaspoon ground cinnamon
1 teaspoon mixed spice
1 teaspoon ground ginger
3 tablespoons pumpkin seeds
3 tablespoons sunflower seeds
butter, for spreading
   and greasing

Topping
1 tablespoon pumpkin seeds
1 tablespoon sunflower seeds
confectioners' sugar, for dusting
   (optional)

Who doesn't love banana bread? Packed full of grated carrots, golden raisins, and seeds, this is a delicious breakfast or snack and a great way to use up overripe bananas.

• •

Preheat the oven to 340°F (170°C), grease a 2 lb loaf pan and line it with parchment paper.

Place all of the ingredients, except the topping, in a large mixing bowl. Mix together with an electric hand-held blender for 1–2 minutes until light and fluffy. Alternatively, use a stand mixer fitted with the paddle or whisk attachment.

Spoon the mixture into the pan and level the top.

Sprinkle with the extra seeds and bake for 1–1¼ hours until golden, well risen, and a skewer inserted comes out clean.

Remove from the oven and let cool on a wire rack, then remove from the pan. Dust with confectioners' sugar (if using), cut into slices, spread with butter, and serve.

Banana Muffins

MAKES 24 MINI MUFFINS

½ cup peeled and mashed ripe
  bananas
½ cup softened unsalted butter
2 eggs
½ cup soft dark brown sugar
1¼ cups self-rising flour
1 teaspoon baking powder
1 teaspoon ground cinnamon
1 teaspoon vanilla extract
¼ cup raisins

Give your little one an energy boost with these mini banana muffins—the perfect finger food for little hands.

Preheat the oven to 350°F (180°C) and line a 24-hole mini muffin pan with mini muffin paper liners.

Place the mashed banana, butter , eggs, sugar, flour, baking powder, cinnamon, and vanilla in a large mixing bowl. Mix together with an electric hand-held blender for 1 minute until light and fluffy, then stir in the raisins. Alternatively, use a stand mixer fitted with the paddle or whisk attachment.

Divide the mixture evenly between the paper liners and bake for 15–18 minutes until well risen and lightly golden. Remove from the oven and let cool on a wire rack.

French Toast

MAKES 2 CHILD PORTIONS
1–2 slices white bread, raisin
   bread, or French bread
1 egg
2 tablespoons whole milk
a generous couple tablespoons
   of unsalted butter or a little
   vegetable oil, for frying

SAVORY FRENCH TOAST
Yeast extract such as Marmite,
   Vegemite, or Promite, for
   spreading (optional)

SWEET FRENCH TOAST
1 tablespoon of fresh orange juice
Light sprinkle of ground
   cinnamon to serve (optional)
Fresh berries or other fruit to
   serve (optional)

French toast served with some fresh berries is a real treat for breakfast. Sprinkle with a little cinnamon and serve with your baby's favorite fruit, or for babies over one you can add a very thin layer of a yeast extract such as Marmite for a savory version.

• •

Remove the crusts from the bread slices and cut each slice into four triangles or into fingers.

For a savory version, spread a thin layer of Marmite or Promite on the bread.

Beat the egg and milk together in a shallow mixing bowl and soak the bread triangles or fingers for a few seconds. Drain on paper towels. Heat the butter or oil in a skillet and fry the soaked bread for 1–2 minutes on each side until lightly golden.

For a sweet version, add a little fresh orange juice and a light sprinkling of ground cinnamon to the egg mixture. Serve immediately with your choice of fruit.

Snacks

Trio of Finger Sandwiches

MAKES 9 FINGER SANDWICHES
3 slices whole-wheat bread
3 slices white bread
a little unsalted butter,
	for spreading

TUNA WITH SWEET CORN
¼ cup drained canned tuna
1 tablespoon mayonnaise
1 tablespoon drained canned
	sweet corn
6 slices cucumber

CLUB SANDWICH
1 tablespoon mayonnaise
¼ cooked chicken breast, sliced
iceberg lettuce, shredded
2 slices Gruyère cheese
½ tomato, sliced
1 hard-boiled egg, sliced

TOMATO, CREAM CHEESE, AND CHIVE
1 tablespoon cream cheese
1 teaspoon chopped chives
½ tomato, sliced

A true lunchtime favorite, sandwiches are the perfect way to start your little ones experimenting with different textures and flavors. Explore these tried-and-tested combos on hungry tums.

• •

Spread all the slices of bread with a little butter and arrange them on a board.

For the tuna mayonnaise and sweet corn sandwich, mix the tuna, mayonnaise, and corn together in a bowl. Spread the mixture over one slice of whole-wheat bread. Top with the cucumber, then sandwich together with a slice of white bread. Remove the crusts and cut into 3 fingers.

For the club sandwich, spread one slice of whole-wheat bread with the mayonnaise. Top with the chicken, lettuce, cheese, tomato, and egg. Sandwich together with a slice of white bread. Remove the crusts and cut into 3 fingers.

For the tomato, cream cheese, and chive sandwich, combine the cream cheese and chives. Spread the mixture over one slice of whole-wheat bread. Top with the sliced tomato. Sandwich together with a slice of white bread. Remove the crusts and cut into 3 fingers.

Dips

Serve these delicious dips with breadsticks, cucumber, carrot, sweet red or yellow bell pepper sticks, pita bread, and cherry tomatoes, and try offering some more unusual vegetables, such as sugar snap peas, too.

• •

Sweet Chili and Cream Cheese Dip

½ cup light cream cheese
1 teaspoon chopped chives
1 teaspoon sweet chili sauce

Mix the cream cheese and chives together and transfer to a small serving dish. Spoon over the chili sauce or mix it into the cream cheese if you prefer.

Thousand Island Dip

2 tablespoons Greek-style yogurt
2 tablespoons mayonnaise
2 teaspoons tomato ketchup
½ teaspoon lemon juice
1–2 drops of Worcestershire sauce

Mix the ingredients together and transfer to a small serving dish.

Ranch Dip

3 tablespoons sour cream
2 tablespoons mayonnaise
1 teaspoon lime or lemon juice (optional)
1 teaspoon chopped cilantro
1 teaspoon chopped chives

Mix the ingredients together and transfer to a small serving dish.

Mango and Cream Cheese Dip

4 tablespoons light cream cheese
3 tablespoons plain yogurt
1½ tablespoons mango chutney
1 tablespoon lemon juice
a pinch of curry powder

Mix all the ingredients together and transfer to a small serving dish.

Cottage Cheese Dip

½ cup cottage cheese
2 tablespoons mayonnaise
4 teaspoons tomato ketchup
squeeze of lemon juice
a tiny drop of Worcestershire sauce (optional)

Process the ingredients in a food processor until smooth. Chill in the refrigerator until ready to serve.

My Favorite Cobb Salad

MAKES 8 CHILD PORTIONS
2 Little Gem lettuces, shredded
1 cup cubed Gruyère cheese
1–2 ripe avocados, halved, pitted,
    peeled, and chopped
3 eggs, hard-boiled and peeled
4 tomatoes, seeded and chopped
2 cooked chicken breasts, cubed
2 slices of crispy cooked smoked
    bacon, chopped (optional)
sprig of basil, to serve

Dressing
1 tablespoon Dijon mustard
2 tablespoons rice wine vinegar
2 tablespoons mirin
2 teaspoons honey or
    maple syrup
6 tablespoons light olive oil
    (or whatever olive oil you
    have on hand)

Little ones love finely chopped salads, and this is one of my all-time favorites. It's good as a light lunch, picnic, or snack. Use maple syrup instead of honey in the dressing, if serving to babies under 12 months, and omit the bacon.

● ●

Arrange all the salad ingredients on a round plate or serving board. Garnish with the basil in the center.

Place all the dressing ingredients in a mixing bowl or jar, and whisk or shake until well blended. Serve the dressing on the side.

Sweet Potato and Parsnip Chips

MAKES 2–3 CHILD PORTIONS
1 small parsnip, peeled
1 small sweet potato, peeled
1 tablespoon olive oil
a small pinch of sea salt
(for babies over 12 months old)

It's no secret that children love potato chips, so it's a good idea to introduce healthier alternatives early on in their weaning. Sweet potatoes and parsnips have a natural sweetness and roasting them in the oven caramelizes them, intensifying that flavor.

• •

Preheat the oven to 400°F (200°C) and line two large baking sheets with parchment paper.

Use a swivel peeler to peel thin strips from the parsnip. Put the strips in a bowl and toss with half the oil. Spread them out in a single layer on one of the lined baking sheets.

Repeat the process with the sweet potato, spreading the strips on the second baking sheet.

Roast the parsnip and sweet potato chips for 10 minutes, then swap the baking sheets around so that the one on the higher oven rack is moved to a lower shelf. You may find that the parsnip cooks slightly faster than the sweet potato, so keep an eye on them because they brown very quickly. Roast for 5 minutes more, or until crisp and browned at the edges, then remove from the oven.

Transfer the chips to a bowl and sprinkle with salt, if using. These are best served the day they are made.

Cheat's Spring Rolls (1+ year) (DAIRY FREE)

MAKES 4 SMALL WRAPS

1 tablespoon sunflower oil

2 boneless, skinless chicken
   breasts, cut into very thin strips

1 medium carrot, peeled and
   coarsely grated

2 handfuls of beansprouts

2 scallions, thinly sliced

1 teaspoon dark soy sauce

2 tablespoons plum sauce

4 small wheat tortilla wraps

Chinese spring rolls are so delicious, but takeout versions are often deep-fried, making them an unhealthy treat. So, I've come up with a healthy, but just as tasty, version that you can make at home, and which are suitable for the little ones.

• •

Preheat the broiler. Heat the oil in a wok or large skillet, add the chicken, and stir-fry it for 2 minutes. Add the vegetables and stir-fry for 2 minutes more, until the chicken has cooked through and the vegetables have softened slightly (but aren't completely soft). Stir in the soy sauce and 1 teaspoon of the plum sauce, and remove from the heat.

Spread the remaining plum sauce over the four wraps. Divide the chicken and vegetable filling between the wraps, spooning it on to the lower half of each wrap. Fold the left- and right-hand sides of the wrap over the filling then roll the wraps up from the bottom, so that the filling is completely enclosed.

Carefully transfer the filled wraps to a broiler pan, placing them seam-side down. Broil for 1–1½ minutes, until the tops are crisp and starting to brown, then turn them over and broil for 1–1½ minutes more. Watch carefully as the wrap can scorch easily. Remove from the broiler and serve immediately.

Tip

★ If the rolls won't stay wrapped, secure them with wooden skewers before you broil them. Remove the skewers before serving.

My First Spanish Omelet

1 tablespoon olive oil
1 small onion, finely chopped
6 new potatoes, cooked and sliced
4 large eggs
2 tablespoons milk
¼ cup grated Parmesan cheese
1 tablespoon chopped basil leaves
8 cherry tomatoes, chopped

Spanish omelet is a great dish to cut into wedges and serve cold, and the eggs provide a good source of iron for your little one. Try swapping the tomatoes for some diced zucchini and red bell pepper, if you like, or other vegetables.

Preheat the broiler to high.

Heat the olive oil in a small skillet about 8 in (20 cm) in diameter, add the onion and sauté for 4–5 minutes, until softened. Add the sliced potatoes and stir to coat them in the oil.

Beat the eggs, milk and cheese together in a bowl or jug. Pour the mixture over the potatoes and onion in the pan and scatter the basil and chopped tomatoes on top.

Cook over a medium heat until the egg mixture has set around the edges of the skillet then place under the broiler for 4–5 minutes until the omelet is set and firm in the middle.

Remove from the broiler and let cool slightly before serving, or serve cold.

Turkey and Cucumber Wraps

DAIRY FREE

MAKES 2 WRAPS

2 small tortilla wraps
2 tablespoons mayonnaise
2 teaspoons sweet chili sauce
4 thin slices cooked turkey
8 thin cucumber julienne

Tip

★ You could swap the turkey for cooked chicken (perhaps leftovers from my Roast Chicken on page 126) or shredded roast duck.

Quick and easy to prepare, these wraps are a snack savior. Turkey is a fantastic source of protein and zinc, which is important for a healthy immune system. The mayonnaise and sweet chili sauce gives the roll-ups a great flavor, too. If you want to try something different, swap the sweet chili sauce for 1½ teaspoons of plum sauce.

• •

Warm the tortilla wraps in the microwave for 20 seconds, then place them on a cutting board.

Combine the mayonnaise and chili sauce and spread the mixture over the wraps. Top each wrap with two turkey slices, add four cucumber julienne next to the turkey, then roll up the wraps so the cucumber is in the middle.

Slice each wrap into bite-sized pieces.

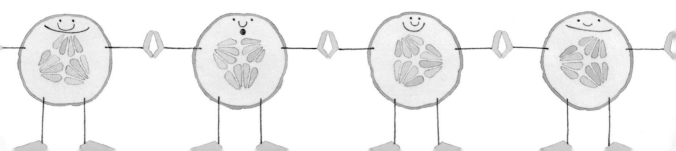

Kebabs

Sometimes the simplest ideas are the most effective in tempting little ones to eat well. Threading colorful bite-sized pieces of food onto a straw or skewer not only makes it fun for children, it offers them a wide variety of nutritious vegetables, too. (If using wooden skewers, remove them before serving to babies and young childen.)

● ●

Chicken Kebabs

MAKES 4 KEBABS

4 oz (100 g) cooked chicken breast,
   cut into 4 large bite-sized pieces
4 thin slices Gruyère cheese
4 cherry tomatoes (if giving to babies under
   one year, cut into halves or quarters)
¼ cucumber, halved, seeded, and
   cut into 4 large chunks

You will also need: 4 plastic straws
   or wooden skewers

Thread a piece of chicken onto a straw. Add a slice of rolled-up cheese, a cherry tomato, and a chunk of cucumber. Repeat, threading the chicken, cheese, tomato, and cucumber onto the remaining straws.

Salad Kebabs

MAKES 4 KEBABS

1 Little Gem lettuce, cut into bite-sized pieces
½ sweet red bell pepper, seeded and
   cut into 1 in (2.5 cm) chunks
¼ cucumber, halved, seeded, and
   cut into 1 in (2.5 cm) chunks
8 cherry tomatoes (if giving to babies under
   one year, cut into halves or quarters)

Creamy Dressing
2 tablespoons rice wine vinegar
1 tablespoon apple juice
⅓ cup light olive oil
2 tablespoons mayonnaise
1 tablespoon cold water
1 tablespoon grated Parmesan cheese

You will also need: 4 plastic straws
   or wooden skewers

Thread a piece of lettuce onto a straw then add a chunk of bell pepper, cucumber, and a cherry tomato. Repeat so you have two pieces of each vegetable on the kebab, then thread the remaining vegetables onto the remaining three straws.

Whisk the dressing ingredients in a bowl and drizzle the dressing over the kebabs.

Serve as a snack with fruit and yogurt.

Arancini ❄

MAKES 12–15 BALLS
2 teaspoons unsalted butter
1 shallot, finely chopped
1 small garlic clove, crushed
½ cup risotto rice
1 cup unsalted or diluted
   chicken stock
¼ cup grated Parmesan cheese
5 tablespoons all-purpose flour
1 egg, beaten
½ cup dried breadcrumbs
sunflower oil for deep frying

Quick Tomato Sauce
olive oil
1 shallot, finely diced
1 garlic clove, crushed
1 x 14.5 oz (411 g) can chopped
   tomatoes
½ teaspoon soft light brown sugar
1 tablespoon tomato ketchup
a little salt and pepper (for
   babies over 12 months old)

These are perfect finger food. The soft middle and crispy breadcrumb coating makes them a great way to introduce different textures.

• •

Melt the butter in a saucepan, add the shallot, and sauté for a few minutes until softened. Then add the garlic and rice and stir for 1 minute. Add the stock, bring to a boil, and stir. Cover and simmer for 15–20 minutes until the rice is just cooked and the stock has been absorbed.

Remove from the heat. Stir in the Parmesan and transfer the risotto to a plate to cool. Once cool, cover and refrigerate for 1 hour.

Heat a little oil for the tomato sauce in a large skillet, add the shallot and garlic, and sauté for 2 minutes. Add the remaining sauce ingredients and bring to a boil, then simmer for 15 minutes, stirring occasionally, until thickened. Season to taste (if using).

Place the flour, beaten egg and breadcrumbs in three separate bowls. Shape the cold risotto into 12–15 balls and coat the balls one at a time, first in the flour, then the egg and finally rolling them in the breadcrumbs.

Heat some sunflower oil in a deep-sided skillet until hot. Fry the balls for about 3 minutes, in batches of 3–4 at a time, until golden and hot through, then drain on paper towels, and serve.

Speedy Crostini

MAKES 12–15 CROSTINI
1 small par-baked baguette
1 tablespoon olive oil
6 tablespoons chopped
   fresh tomatoes
1½ tablespoons sun-dried
   tomato paste
5 basil leaves, chopped
10 cherry tomatoes, sliced
½ cup grated Cheddar cheese
a little salt and pepper (for
   babies over 12 months old)

Who doesn't love crostini? This simple classic is easy to make at home and sure to be a hit. Why not get your child involved in adding the fresh cherry tomato and basil topping.

• •

Preheat the oven to 350°F (180°C) and line a baking sheet with parchment paper.

Remove the ends of the baguette and cut it into roughly ¾ in (1.5 cm)slices, then brush the slices with olive oil and place them on the baking sheet. Bake for 10 minutes until lightly golden and crisp.

Mix the tomatoes, sundried tomato paste, and some seasoning (if using) together in a bowl. Spoon the mixture on top of the baked bread slices and arrange the basil, cherry tomatoes, and cheese on top. Bake for 10–12 minutes until golden and the cheese has melted.

Topping Variations

Avocado and tomato: Mash 1 ripe avocado, spread on the toasted baguette slices, and top with chopped tomatoes.

Chicken and pesto: Combine 1 chopped chicken breast with 2 tablespoons of mayonnaise and 1 teaspoon of pesto and spread over the baguette slices.

Salmon and cream cheese: Spread cream cheese on the baguette slices and top with strips of smoked salmon.

Vegetables

Cauliflower in Breadcrumbs

1 large cauliflower, cut into florets
½ cup all-purpose flour
2 eggs, beaten
2 tablespoons milk
¾ cup dried breadcrumbs
⅓ cup grated Parmesan cheese
1 tablespoon chopped fresh thyme
   (optional)
a little salt and pepper (for
   babies over 12 months old)

Roasted cauliflower florets with a crisp cheesy coating is an irresistible melt-in-the-mouth combination. Sometimes, the key to encouraging a child to accept certain foods is about preparing them in different ways. For example, a lot of kids I know wouldn't eat boiled cauliflower, but roasting it changes everything!

Preheat the oven to 400°F (200°C) and line a baking sheet with parchment paper.

Put the flour in a large plastic baggie and add seasoning (if using). Add the cauliflower florets and shake to coat them in the flour.

Beat the eggs and milk together in a mixing bowl, and put the breadcrumbs, cheese, and thyme (if using) in a second plastic baggie, shaking to combine the ingredients. Remove the cauliflower florets from the first baggie and dip them into the egg, then add them to the breadcrumbs and shake to coat.

Place the cauliflower florets on the lined baking sheet and roast for 25–30 minutes, until golden and crisp. Remove from the oven and serve right away. I like to serve them with fish goujons (see my Crispy Fish Fingers recipe on page 147), chicken fingers, mini meatballs, chicken balls, or salmon balls (see my Salmon, Quinoa, and Spinach Balls recipe on page 158).

Green Macaroni ✳

MAKES 4 CHILD PORTIONS
1⅓ cup macaroni
1 tablespoon butter
2 tablespoons all-purpose flour
1¼ cups milk, warmed
½ teaspoon Dijon mustard
½ cup grated aged
   Cheddar cheese
1 cup finely chopped fresh spinach

Fussiness often strikes when it comes to serving up anything green. However, my special green macaroni always wins over the doubters!

• •

Cook the macaroni according to the package instructions, then drain.

Melt the butter in a saucepan. Add the flour and stir over the heat for 1 minute, then gradually add the milk, whisking constantly, until you have a smooth, thick sauce. Remove from the heat, add the mustard, cheese, and spinach, and stir until the cheese has melted.

Add the cooked macaroni and stir until thoroughly warmed through. Serve with salad or cucumber and carrot sticks.

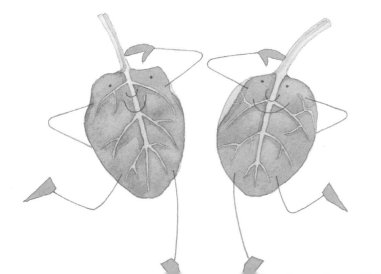

Parmesan Roasted Sweet Potato Wedges

MAKES 4 CHILD PORTIONS

1 lb 8 oz (800 g) sweet potatoes, scrubbed and cut into thick wedges or chunky fries

2 tablespoons olive oil

1 tablespoon cornstarch

2 tablespoons finely grated Parmesan cheese

3 large sage leaves, chopped (optional)

a little salt and pepper (for babies over 12 months old)

Babies love the flavor of these baked sweet potato "steak fries," coated with Parmesan and sage. Roasting sweet potato intensifies the natural sweetness. Make sure they are cut large enough for a child to hold easily in their fist so that one end sticks out. This recipe can be lightly seasoned.

• •

Preheat the oven to 400°F (200°C).

Place the sweet potato wedges on a baking sheet. Add the oil and cornstarch and toss to coat. Season with salt and pepper (if using).

Place in the oven and roast for 20 minutes, turning them over after 15 minutes. Add the Parmesan and sage (if using) and put them back in the oven for 3–4 minutes until the cheese has melted.

I like to serve these with fish goujons (see my Crispy Fish Fingers recipe on page 147), chicken fingers, mini meatballs, chicken balls, or salmon balls (see my Salmon, Quinoa, and Spinach Balls recipe on page 158).

Lentil Dal ❄

MAKES 6 CHILD PORTIONS

2 tablespoons sunflower oil
1 large onion, chopped
3 small carrots, peeled and cubed
1 sweet red bell pepper, seeded
   and cubed
3 garlic cloves, crushed
a pinch of dried chili flakes
2 teaspoons mild curry paste
2 teaspoons garam masala
½ cup yellow split peas
3 cups unsalted or diluted
   vegetable stock
⅓ cup frozen peas
2 tablespoons crème fraîche or
   heavy cream
squeeze of lemon

It's important to introduce a world of flavor to your baby early on, so this recipe is the perfect introduction to curry and mild spices. Lentils are also a good source of protein, iron, and fiber, all of which are important for your baby's development. It's quite thick and sticks to the spoon, which is helpful when a baby's aim isn't always perfect!

• •

Heat the oil in a saucepan, add the onion, carrot, and pepper, and fry for 2–3 minutes until softened. Add the garlic, chili flakes, curry paste, and garam masala. Stir-fry for 30 seconds, then add the split peas and stock.

Cover with a lid and bring to a boil, then reduce the heat and gently simmer for 1 hour, or until the lentils are soft. Add the peas, crème fraîche, and lemon juice, stir and simmer for 4 minutes more.

Remove from the heat and serve with vegetable sticks and pita bread, and some salad if wished.

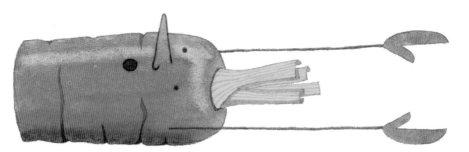

Kale and Veggie Mash

2 teaspoons sunflower oil
⅔ cup chopped onion
1 cup chopped peeled carrots
1 cup chopped peeled potato
¼ cup finely chopped celery
⅓ cup chopped peeled parsnip
1½ cups unsalted or diluted
   vegetable stock
2 teaspoons chopped fresh thyme
   (or ¼ teaspoon dried thyme)
½ cup chopped trimmed kale

Kale is a culinary superhero, full of essential vitamins and minerals like iron and potassium. A good starting point with leafy greens is to combine them with sweet root vegetables or a cheese sauce.

Heat the oil in a saucepan, add the onion, carrot, potato, celery, and parsnip. Cook, stirring, for 2–3 minutes, until softened, then add the stock and thyme. Cover with a lid, bring to a boil, then lower the heat and simmer for 15 minutes.

Add the kale and simmer for 5 minutes more. Remove from the heat and mash.

I like to serve the mash with Chicken and Sweet Corn Croquettes (see page 134), Swedish Meatballs (see page 175), or Chicken and Kale Balls (see page 113).

My Quinoa Salad

DAIRY FREE

MAKES 6 CHILD PORTIONS

1½ cups cooked red and white quinoa (or ¾ cup dried quinoa)

¾ cup drained canned sweet corn,

½ sweet red bell pepper, seeded and diced

4 scallions, finely sliced

4 tablespoons chopped cashew nuts (optional)

3 tablespoons raisins or golden raisins

freshly chopped parsley, to garnish

a little salt and pepper (for babies over 12 months old)

Dressing

2 tablespoons balsamic vinegar

½ garlic clove, crushed

a pinch of sugar

6 tablespoons light olive oil

If using dried quinoa, rinse it in a sieve under cold running water before following the instructions on the package. Once it is cooked and all the water has been absorbed, remove from the heat and leave uncovered for about 5 minutes, then fluff up the quinoa with a fork.

• •

Add the remaining ingredients to the quinoa and season with salt and pepper (if using).

Mix all of the dressing ingredients together in a bowl, pour over the salad, and stir to combine.

Refrigerate for 30 minutes, then garnish with parsley to serve.

I like to serve this salad with my Sweet Corn Fritters (see page 72) or Grilled Vegetable Kebabs (see page 79).

Tomato and Vegetable Soup with Orzo Pasta ❄

MAKES 6 CHILD PORTIONS
1 tablespoon olive oil
⅔ cup cubed peeled carrots
1 cup cubed peeled butternut
   squash
1 onion, chopped
1 garlic clove, crushed
1 tablespoon tomato puree
1 x 14.5 oz (411 g) can chopped
   tomatoes
2 cups unsalted or diluted
   vegetable stock
2–3 tablespoons apple juice
3 tablespoons heavy cream
½ cup orzo pasta
a little salt and pepper (for
   babies over 12 months old)

This is a delicious way to disguise veggies! The orzo (rice-shaped pasta) adds texture to the tasty tomato soup while also remaining nice and soft, so easy for your baby to chew.

• •

Heat the oil in a saucepan. Add the carrot, squash, and onion, and fry for 3–4 minutes, then add the garlic and fry for 30 seconds.

Add the tomato puree, chopped tomatoes, stock, and apple juice. Cover with a lid, bring to a boil, then lower heat and simmer for 15 minutes or until all the vegetables are tender. Remove from the heat and blend until smooth using a hand-held blender. Add the cream and salt and pepper (if using).

Cook the orzo according to the package instructions until just firm. Drain and sprinkle on top of the soup to serve. Serve with salad and fresh bread.

Fusilli with Spinach and Spring Vegetables

MAKES 4 CHILD PORTIONS

1 cup mini fusilli pasta

¼ cup broccoli florets

1 tablespoon olive oil

½ onion, finely chopped

⅝ cup cubed zucchini

¼ cup seeded and cubed sweet red bell pepper

1 garlic clove, crushed

1 cup chopped baby spinach

½ cup unsalted or diluted vegetable stock

3 tablespoons heavy cream

¼ cup grated Parmesan cheese

1 tablespoon chopped basil

a little salt and pepper (for babies over 12 months old)

This simple dish is brimming with veggies and will help toward your family's 5-a-day! If you are bringing up your baby on a vegetarian diet, check the Parmesan you use is made with animal-free rennet. Alternatively, choose another Italian-style hard cheese without animal rennet.

• •

Cook the pasta according to the package instructions. Add the broccoli florets for the last 2 minutes of the cooking time and drain.

Heat the oil in a skillet. Add the onion, zucchini, bell pepper, and garlic, and fry for 3–4 minutes. Add the spinach, cooked pasta, and broccoli, and toss together. Add the stock and cream, bring to a boil, then remove from the heat.

Add the Parmesan and gently fold it through. Sprinkle with the chopped basil to serve and season to taste (if using).

Thai Rice Veggie Wraps

DAIRY FREE

MAKES 6 WRAPS

6 Thai rice paper wrappers

2 x ¾ in (2 cm) pieces
   of cucumber, finely
   sliced lengthwise

2 x ¾ in (2 cm) pieces of peeled
   carrot, finely sliced lengthwise

¼ sweet red bell pepper, finely
   sliced lengthwise into
   ¾ in (2 cm) strips

1 scallion, cut into ¾ in
   (2 cm) pieces and finely
   sliced lengthwise

½ small tub mustard cress

Dip

½ teaspoon fish sauce

2 teaspoons sweet chili sauce

1 tablespoon sunflower oil

2 teaspoons rice wine vinegar

¼ teaspoon grated fresh
   ginger

Don't be afraid to try out new tastes on your child. These rice paper wrappers are full of crunchy veggies and the dipping sauce is a fantastic introduction to Thai-style flavors. Rice paper wrappers for spring rolls are available in specialist oriental stores and large supermarkets.

• •

Soak the wrappers in warm water for a few seconds, one at a time, then place them on a dry plate.

Arrange a mixture of sliced vegetables and cress in the middle of one of the wrappers. Carefully fold in the sides and roll up to make a neat package. Repeat with the remaining five wrappers.

Combine all of the dip ingredients in a small bowl and mix well.

Cheese and Cherry Tomato Muffins ❄

MAKES 12 MUFFINS

1¾ cups self-rising flour
1 teaspoon baking powder
1 tablespoon snipped chives
5 scallions, finely sliced
¾ cup grated aged Cheddar
   cheese
⅜ cup grated Parmesan cheese
¼ cup crumbled feta cheese
1 large egg
⅞ cup buttermilk
⅓ cup sunflower oil
10 cherry tomatoes,
   roughly chopped
freshly ground black pepper

This is a fantastic quick and easy savory muffin recipe, great for a snack on the go or a delicious lunch. Cheese is a good source of calcium, protein, and vitamins A, D, and B12.

Preheat the oven to 325°F (160°C) and line a 12-hole muffin tray with paper liners.

Sift the flour and baking powder into a mixing bowl and add the chives, scallion, and cheeses. Season with a little pepper.

Mix the egg, buttermilk, and oil together in a separate mixing bowl.

Add the wet ingredients to the bowl of dry ingredients and gently mix.

Divide the muffin mixture evenly between the paper liners, top with the chopped tomatoes, and bake for 25–30 minutes until well risen and lightly golden.

Remove from the oven and transfer the muffins in their paper liners to a wire rack to cool (they will deflate slightly). Store in an airtight container for up to 2 days.

Sweet Corn Fritters

MAKES ABOUT
20 SMALL FRITTERS

1 cup drained canned sweet corn
¾ cup whole-wheat flour
1 teaspoon baking powder
2 large eggs
3 tablespoons sweet chili sauce
4 scallions, roughly chopped
handful of basil, chopped
10 cherry tomatoes,
    roughly chopped
1 cup grated halloumi cheese
sunflower oil for frying
a little salt and pepper (for
    babies over 12 months old)

★ These are best served right away
but you can save half the batter and
keep it in the refrigerator to cook
the next day.

Fritters are a firm family favorite and a great way to encourage kids to eat their veggies. Halloumi cheese has a very high melting point so it works well in a fritter. The fresh basil and sweet chili sauce gives these a delicious flavor.

Blend half of the sweet corn in the bowl of a food processor, or in a mixing bowl with a hand-held stick blender, until finely chopped.

Combine the flour, baking powder, and eggs in a bowl. Whisk in the sweet chili sauce and finely chopped sweet corn. Add the remaining ingredients including the remaining whole, unblended corn kernels. Season to taste (if using).

Heat a little oil in a skillet. When hot, fry heaping tablespoonfuls of the fritter mixture for 1–2 minutes on each side until golden and cooked through. Transfer to paper towels, fry the remaining batter, then serve with salad, such as My Quinoa Salad (see page 65).

Curried Vegetable Fritters

DAIRY FREE

MAKES ABOUT
20 SMALL FRITTERS

2 cups coarsely grated peeled
    sweet potato
1½ cups coarsely grated peeled
    carrot
4 scallions, chopped
8 tablespoons cooked quinoa
1 tablespoon chopped cilantro
2 eggs, beaten
6 tablespoons all-purpose flour
1 tablespoon mild curry powder
sunflower oil for frying
a little salt and pepper (for
    babies over 12 months old)

These fritters are so easy to make and are very crave-worthy. The mild curry powder adds a mild, spicy flavor.

• •

Combine the grated sweet potato and carrot in a bowl with the scallion, quinoa, and cilantro. Season with salt and pepper (if using). Add the eggs, then add the flour and curry powder, and mix together until combined.

Heat a little oil in a skillet. When hot, fry heaping tablespoonfuls of the mixture for 2 minutes on each side, flattening the mixture down with a palette knife, until each side until golden.

Transfer to paper towels, fry the remaining batter, then serve with a salad, such as My Quinoa Salad (see page 65), or with Sweet Dijon Chicken Kebabs (see page 112).

Hidden Vegetable Frittata

MAKES 6 CHILD PORTIONS

1 cup diced zucchini

⅓ cup seeded and diced sweet red bell pepper

⅔ cup chopped broccoli (including trimmed stalks)

4 scallions, sliced

5 large eggs

4 tablespoons milk

⅜ cup grated Parmesan cheese

1 tablespoon chopped fresh basil

2 tablespoons butter

2 tablespoons sunflower oil

a little salt and pepper (for babies over 12 months old)

Eggs form the base of this family-friendly frittata, making it an excellent source of protein, iron, and zinc. Packed full of colorful veggies, my children (now all grown up) used to love—and still love—this frittata. As well as adding tons of flavor, the Parmesan seasons the dish.

• •

Put all the vegetables in the bowl of a food processor and process until finely chopped.

Mix the eggs, milk, Parmesan, basil, and a little salt and pepper (if using) together in a large mixing bowl.

Add the finely chopped vegetables to the egg mixture and stir to combine.

Preheat the broiler to high.

Melt the butter and oil in a medium skillet. When the butter starts to foam, add the frittata mixture. Cook, without stirring, until the egg starts to set around the edges, then place the pan under the broiler. Broil for 8–10 minutes until the frittata is set in the middle.

Slide the frittata onto a plate and cut it into wedges. Serve with halved cherry tomatoes and cucumber.

Kale and Tomato Omelet

MAKES 2–3 CHILD PORTIONS

½ cup chopped trimmed kale

2 tablespoons butter

3 scallions, sliced

3 large eggs

2 tablespoons milk

2 tomatoes, diced

2 tablespoons grated
　Parmesan cheese

The combination of eggs, kale, and tomatoes in this omelet packs a nutritious punch, and it can be served for breakfast, lunch, or dinner.

• •

Blanch the kale in boiling water for 4 minutes, then drain and refresh under cold running water. Drain and squeeze out the water.

Heat a non-stick omelet pan or small skillet until hot. Add the butter and, as soon as it starts to foam, add the scallions and blanched kale and fry for 2 minutes.

Beat the eggs and milk together, then add them to the pan. Stir until the mixture is set underneath. Sprinkle with the tomatoes and cheese, cook for about 1 minute, then fold in half.

Cook for 3–4 minutes more, until the inside is cooked through and the outside is lightly golden.

Remove from the pan and cut into 4 pieces. Serve right away.

Eggplant Pasta ❄

MAKES 6 CHILD PORTIONS
2½ cups fusilli pasta
2 tablespoons sunflower oil
1 red onion, chopped
2 garlic cloves, crushed
1 mild red chili, seeded and diced
  (optional)
1 eggplant, cubed
1 x 14.5 oz (411 g) can chopped
  tomatoes
1 tablespoon tomato puree
1 cup unsalted or diluted
  vegetable stock
a pinch of sugar
a handful of fresh basil, chopped
½ cup grated Parmesan cheese

Eggplants are rich in antioxidants and are a great source of dietary fiber. With a hint of chili and a sprinkling of Parmesan, this pasta dish is comfort food at its best.

• •

Cook the pasta according to the package instructions, then drain.

While the pasta is cooking, heat the oil in a skillet, add the onion, garlic, and chili (if using), and fry for 2–3 minutes until the onion and garlic have softened. Add the eggplant and fry over a high heat for 4–5 minutes more, then add the chopped tomatoes, tomato puree, and stock. Simmer for 5 minutes.

Remove the skillet from the heat and add the cooked pasta along with the basil and Parmesan, and toss together. Serve with cucumber and carrot.

Grilled Vegetable Kebabs

MAKES 4 KEBABS

1 garlic clove, crushed
½ teaspoon soy sauce
½ teaspoon maple syrup
2 teaspoons chopped fresh thyme
1 tablespoon light olive oil,
    plus extra for greasing
8 small cauliflower florets
8 cherry tomatoes
4 baby zucchinis, each cut
    into 4 pieces
½ sweet red bell pepper, seeded
    and cut into 8 pieces
8 button mushrooms

You will also need: 4 wooden
    skewers, soaked in warm
    water for 30 minutes

The trick to making these kebabs super-tasty is my marinade. Using a little soy, thyme, and maple syrup makes them sweet, sticky, and succulent.

Preheat the broiler to high. Line a baking sheet with foil and lightly grease with olive oil.

Combine the garlic, soy sauce, maple syrup, thyme, and oil in a bowl. Add the vegetables and coat them in the marinade, then set aside to marinate for 5 minutes.

Thread the vegetables onto the soaked skewers and arrange on the baking sheet. Place under the broiler for 5 minutes on each side until lightly golden and cooked through. Remove from the broiler and let cool slightly before serving, removing the skewers for toddlers and children.

Tasty Veggie Burrito

MAKES 1 BURRITO
(2 CHILD PORTIONS)

1 soft tortilla wrap (about
   8 in (20 cm) in diameter)
1 egg
1 tablespoon butter
½ red onion, finely chopped
½ sweet red bell pepper, seeded
   and diced
leaves from 1 sprig of thyme
a pinch of paprika
1 tomato, seeded and diced
2–3 drops of Tabasco sauce
   (optional)
¼ cup grated Cheddar cheese
1 tablespoon sour cream, to serve
   (optional)
a little salt and pepper (for
   babies over 12 months old)

Tip

★ If you prefer, cut the omelet
into little strips and mix it in with
the cooked onion and red bell
pepper mixture.

It's good to get together at mealtimes, and my veggie-packed burritos can easily be doubled in quantity to serve the whole family: simply make two separate omelets and double the filling quantities.

• •

Put the tortilla on a large plate. Beat the egg with 1 teaspoon of water and a little salt and pepper.

Heat half of the butter in an 8-in (20-cm) non-stick skillet. Add the egg and tilt the pan to help the egg spread out and make a thin omelet. Cook for 2–3 minutes, until the omelet has set, then slide it onto the tortilla.

Heat the remaining butter in the skillet and, once it starts to foam, add the onion, red bell pepper, thyme, and paprika and sauté for 5 minutes, until the onion and pepper are soft. Add the tomato and cook for 2 minutes more, until the tomato is soft.

Add the Tabasco sauce (if using) and season with salt and pepper (if using). Remove from the heat and set aside for a moment.

Heat the tortilla and omelet for 10–20 seconds in a microwave, spoon the pepper and onion mixture over the center, sprinkle over the cheese, and roll it up. Serve immediately with a spoonful of sour cream, if you wish.

Veggie Balls ❄

MAKES 15 VEGGIE BALLS
⅓ cup dried breadcrumbs
½ cup grated carrot
4 scallions, chopped
½ cup chopped brown mushrooms
⅜ cup grated Parmesan cheese
1 tablespoon chopped fresh basil
1 teaspoon chopped fresh thyme
2 teaspoons soy sauce
1 teaspoon sweet chili sauce
1–2 tablespoons all-purpose flour
2 tablespoons sunflower oil
a little salt and pepper (for
    babies over 12 months old)

These little balls are a fantastic way to pack in veggies and are ideal finger food. They are also perfect for batch-cooking and freezing. Just store them in a plastic freezer container, separating each layer with wax paper, and reheat from frozen in the oven or microwave when needed.

Prick the potato and bake it in the microwave for 7–10 minutes until soft. Let cool, then cut it in half and scoop out the flesh—you will need about ¾ cup of potato in total.

Put the cool potato and remaining ingredients (except the flour and the oil) in a food processor and process until combined. Transfer the mixture to a bowl, season lightly with salt and pepper (if using), and shape into 15 equal-sized balls.

Place the flour in a bowl and lightly coat the balls. Transfer them to a plate and refrigerate for 15 minutes.

Heat the oil in a skillet until hot. Fry the balls for about 2 minutes until golden all over and heated through. Serve with cucumber and halved cherry tomatoes, or a mayonnaise dip with sweet chili sauce.

Rice and Vegetable Croquettes

MAKES 12 CROQUETTES
¾ cup cold cooked white
    or brown rice
½ cup grated peeled carrot
3 tablespoons seeded and finely
    diced sweet red bell pepper
¼ cup grated zucchini
5 scallions, chopped
⅓ cup grated Parmesan cheese
1 small egg, beaten
¼ cup dried breadcrumbs, plus
    extra for dusting
2 teaspoons sweet chili sauce
1 tablespoon chopped fresh basil
1 teaspoon soy sauce
2 tablespoons light olive oil
a little salt and pepper (for
    babies over 12 months old)

These veggie-packed croquettes can be made with leftover rice and are a great way to make sure your little one gets their five-a-day.

• •

Put the rice, carrot, bell pepper, zucchini, scallion, and Parmesan in a food processor and process until roughly chopped. Add the egg and breadcrumbs, sweet chili sauce, basil, and soy sauce. Process again until finely chopped.

Transfer the mixture to a bowl, season lightly with salt and pepper (if using), and shape into 12 equal-sized croquettes. Place some extra breadcrumbs on a large plate and coat the croquettes with the breadcrumbs. Refrigerate the croquettes if you have time, to help them keep their shape (this is not essential).

Heat the oil in a skillet until hot. Fry the croquettes for 2 minutes on each side until lightly golden and crisp, and heated through. Serve with a chopped salad or crudités with a dip (see page 41 for dip ideas).

Roasted Veggie Ratatouille

DAIRY FREE

MAKES 4–6 CHILD PORTIONS
½ eating apple, peeled,
   cored, and diced
1 large zucchini, diced
1 sweet red bell pepper, seeded
   and diced
2 tablespoons olive oil
1 red onion, chopped
1 garlic clove, crushed
1 x 14.5 oz (411 g) can chopped
   tomatoes
2 teaspoons tomato puree
½ teaspoon maple syrup
1 tablespoon chopped fresh basil
   (optional)
a little salt and pepper (for
   babies over 12 months old)

Roasting vegetables intensifies their natural
sweetness and this is a delicious way to get
your baby to love veggies.

Preheat the oven to 350°F (180°C).

Put the apple, zucchini, and bell pepper in a roasting
pan, drizzle with half the oil, and toss together. Roast
for 15 minutes.

Meanwhile, heat the remaining oil in a saucepan,
add the onion and garlic, and fry for 2 minutes until
softened. Add the tomatoes, tomato puree, ½ cup of
water, and the maple syrup, and bring to a boil. Add
the roasted vegetables, cover, and simmer for 15
minutes until reduced and softened.

Remove from the heat, season with salt and pepper
(if using), and add the basil to serve, if you wish.

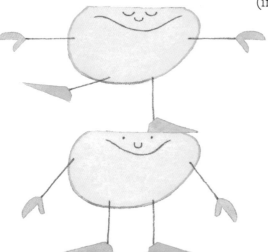

Squash, Spinach, and Ricotta Risotto

MAKES 4 CHILD PORTIONS

1¼ cups cubed peeled butternut squash
½ tablespoon chopped fresh thyme
2 tablespoons olive oil
1 onion, finely diced
1 garlic clove, crushed
½ cup risotto rice
2 teaspoons white wine vinegar
1⅔ cups unsalted or diluted hot vegetable stock
1 cup chopped spinach
a pinch of grated nutmeg
¼ cup grated Parmesan cheese
1 tablespoon ricotta cheese
a little salt and pepper (for babies over 12 months old)

Combined cooked rice and vegetables make a soft meal, and is a good way to introduce texture to your baby's food. Butternut squash is rich in vitamin A, calcium, and potassium, and its natural sweetness paired with creamy ricotta and fresh thyme, is a match made in heaven.

• •

Preheat the oven to 400°F (200°C).

Toss the squash with the thyme and 1 tablespoon of the oil in a roasting pan and roast for 20 minutes, or until soft and golden.

Heat the rest of the oil in a saucepan, add the onion, and fry for 5 minutes until softened, then add the garlic and fry for 30 seconds more. Add the rice and stir to coat it in the oil, then add the vinegar and stir for 10 seconds. Add the stock, bring to a boil, cover with a lid, lower heat, and simmer gently for 15 minutes until the rice is just cooked and all the stock has been absorbed.

Add the spinach, nutmeg, cheeses, and roasted squash to the pan while it's still over the heat. Lightly season with salt and pepper (if using), and stir until the spinach has wilted.

Serve immediately with steamed vegetables, such as broccoli florets.

Butternut Squash Rice

MAKES 4 CHILD PORTIONS
2 tablespoons butter
⅓ cup finely chopped onion
1 garlic clove, crushed
½ cup basmati rice
2 cups boiling water
1 cup cubed peeled
    butternut squash
3 ripe tomatoes, skinned,
    seeded, and chopped
½ cup grated Cheddar cheese
1 tablespoon chopped fresh basil

A simple but delicious rice dish with butternut squash and a fresh tomato and cheese sauce.

•••••••••••••••••••••••••••••••••••

Heat half the butter in a saucepan, add the onion, and sauté for 3–4 minutes until softened, then add the garlic and cook for 30 seconds more. Add the rice and stir to coat it in the butter. Pour over the boiling water, cover with a lid, and cook for 8 minutes over a high heat. Stir in the chopped butternut squash, reduce the heat, and cook, covered, for 12 more minutes or until all the water has been absorbed.

Meanwhile, melt the remaining butter in a small saucepan, add the chopped tomatoes and sauté for 2–3 minutes. Stir in the cheese until melted, then add the cheese and tomato mixture to the rice and stir it through.

Serve with steamed broccoli florets or Cauliflower in Breadcrumbs (see page 58).

Pasta

Chicken Pasta Salad

DAIRY FREE

MAKES 4 CHILD PORTIONS
1 cup shelled edamame
2 cups cooked baby shell pasta
¾ cup quartered cherry tomatoes
¾ cup drained tinned sweet corn
1 cup diced cooked chicken
   breast

Dressing
2 tablespoons rice wine vinegar
1 tablespoon honey or maple
   syrup
1 tablespoon soy sauce
4 tablespoons mild olive oil

This recipe is an all-around winner; babies love the bright colors and the size of the vegetables and mini pasta. This looks great in layers but for little ones it's best to mix the ingredients together and serve it in a child-safe bowl (not glass). Broccoli florets make a good alternative to the edamame, if you want to switch the ingredients. Use maple syrup in the dressing instead of honey if serving to babies under 12 months old.

• •

Cook the edamame in a pan of boiling water for 5 minutes until tender. Drain and refresh under cold running water.

Layer the ingredients in jars or bowls, starting with the cooked pasta, followed by the tomatoes, sweet corn, cooked edamame, and finally the diced chicken.

Mix the dressing ingredients together in a small mixing bowl and serve with the salad.

Pasta, Chicken, and Veggie Salad

MAKES 4 CHILD PORTIONS

1¼ cups macaroni
⅔ cup sliced green beans
½ sweet red bell pepper, seeded
    and diced
4 scallions, sliced
6 cherry tomatoes, quartered
1 cooked chicken breast, diced
a little salt and pepper (for
    babies over 12 months old)

Dressing
1 teaspoon Dijon mustard
2 teaspoons rice wine vinegar
2 tablespoons light olive oil
1 teaspoon honey or maple syrup
1 tablespoon red pesto

Quick to prepare and packed with protein and carbohydrates, this salad will keep your baby fueled for a busy day. Use maple syrup instead of honey in the dressing, if serving to babies under 12 months.

• •

Cook the macaroni according to the package instructions. Add the green beans 4 minutes before the end of the cooking time. Drain and refresh under cold running water.

Combine the cooked macaroni and green beans with the bell pepper, scallions, tomatoes, and chicken in a serving bowl.

Whisk the dressing ingredients together in a separate mixing bowl, then pour over the pasta and season lightly with salt and pepper (if using).

Whole-wheat Pasta with Ham and Broccoli

MAKES 4 CHILD PORTIONS

1 cup whole-wheat fusilli
 pasta or other pasta shape
½ cup broccoli florets
½ cup diced cooked ham
½ cup mini mozzarella balls
6 cherry tomatoes, quartered
¼ cucumber, peeled and diced
a little salt and pepper (for
 babies over 12 months old)

Dressing
1½ tablespoons rice wine vinegar
3 tablespoons light olive oil
1 teaspoon soy sauce
1 teaspoon maple syrup

Whole-wheat pasta is a good source of complex carbs; it's digested at a slower pace so helps sustain energy levels for longer. Little ones will also love the tasty ham and mini mozzarella balls in this dish. You could add diced Gruyère cheese instead of mozzarella if your child prefers.

Cook the pasta according to the package instructions. Add the broccoli florets 3 minutes before the end of the cooking time. Drain and refresh under cold running water.

Mix the cooled, cooked pasta and broccoli in a serving bowl with the ham, mozzarella balls, tomatoes, and diced cucumber.

Whisk the dressing ingredients together in a separate mixing bowl, then pour over the pasta. Season with a little salt and pepper (if using).

Hidden Vegetable Tomato Sauce

MAKES 4–5 CHILD PORTIONS

2 teaspoons canola,
  sunflower, or olive oil
½ cup chopped peeled carrot
⅓ cup chopped zucchini
⅔ cup chopped onion
½ apple, peeled, cored, and diced
2 garlic cloves
21 oz (2⅔ cups) canned chopped
  tomatoes
1 tablespoon sun-dried
  tomato paste
1 tablespoon tomato puree
1 cup unsalted or diluted
  vegetable stock
½ cup apple juice
1 tablespoon torn fresh
  basil leaves

Pasta with a tomato sauce is always a winner—my secret ingredient is the apple, which brings out a hint of sweetness in the tomato sauce and takes away any acidity. I blend the ingredients for reluctant veggie eaters, as what they can't see, they can't pick out. This also makes a great sauce to go with my Swedish Meatballs or Chicken and Kale Balls (see pages 175 and 113).

• •

Heat the oil in a saucepan, add the vegetables, apple, and garlic, and fry for about 4 minutes, until softened. Add the tomatoes, stock, and apple juice. Bring to a boil, then reduce the heat and simmer for 20 minutes, stirring occasionally, until the vegetables are tender. Remove from the heat, add the basil, and process until smooth using a hand-held stick blender.

Serve with pasta.

Animal Pasta with Broccoli

1 cup animal pasta shapes
   (or letters or stars)
½ cup broccoli florets
1 tablespoon olive oil
½ large zucchini, diced
1 garlic clove, peeled and
   crushed
4 ripe tomatoes, quartered
2 tablespoons drained canned
   sweet corn
1 tablespoon butter
⅓ cup grated Parmesan cheese

Sometimes it can be a challenge to get fussy eaters to eat anything else except pasta with a little butter and grated cheese, but if anything will persuade them to eat their greens, this simple recipe—with the addition of little broccoli "trees" and colorful veggies—will.

• •

Cook the pasta according to the package instructions, adding the broccoli florets 3 minutes before the end of the cooking time. Reserve 6 tablespoons of the cooking water before draining the pasta.

Heat the oil in a small skillet. Add the zucchini and garlic and fry for 3 minutes, making sure the garlic doesn't burn, then add the tomatoes and corn. Add the pasta and broccoli and toss together. Add the reserved pasta cooking water, then remove the skillet from the heat and set aside for 3–4 minutes. Add the butter and cheese and gently mix through until melted.

Pasta with Tomato and Mascarpone Sauce ❄

MAKES 4 CHILD PORTIONS

1 tablespoon olive oil

1 red onion, chopped

¼ cup diced peeled carrot

¼ cup zucchini, diced

⅛ cup diced celery

1 garlic clove, crushed

½ cup chopped button
   mushrooms

14 oz passata, tomato sauce, or
   canned chopped tomatoes

2 tablespoons apple juice

⅔ cup mini pasta shells

2 tablespoons torn basil leaves
   (optional)

3 tablespoons mascarpone

3 tablespoons grated
   Parmesan cheese

★ If freezing, freeze the sauce
separately, before you mix it
with the pasta.

Five different vegetables are blended into this tasty tomato sauce. If you can't find the slightly thicker passata, use tomato sauce, which is readily available. Mascarpone is good for babies as they need proportionately more fat in their diets than adults due to their rapid growth rate. If you don't have any, use heavy cream or regular cream cheese instead.

• •

Heat the oil in a saucepan, add the onion, carrot, zucchini, and celery, and sauté for 5 minutes. Add the garlic and sauté for a minute more, then add the mushrooms and sauté for 2 minutes. Stir in the passata or tomato sauce with the apple juice, then cover and simmer for 10 minutes, stirring occasionally.

Meanwhile, cook the pasta shells according to the package instructions, and drain.

Remove the tomato sauce from the heat, add the basil (if using), let cool slightly, then blend in a food processor or directly in the saucepan using a hand-held stick blender. Return to the pan (if using the processor) and stir in the mascarpone and Parmesan. Stir the sauce into the drained pasta and serve. This dish goes well with my Chicken and Kale Balls (see page 113).

Variation: Chicken, tomato, and mascarpone

Add ½ cup diced cooked chicken breast at the same time as the mushrooms.

Tomato, Sweet Potato, and Cheese Sauce with Pasta Shells ❄

MAKES 4 CHILD PORTIONS

1 tablespoon olive oil

1 onion, chopped

1 garlic clove, crushed

1½ cups chopped peeled sweet potatoes

2 medium carrots, peeled and sliced

1 x 14.5 oz (411 g) can chopped tomatoes

1 cup unsalted or diluted vegetable stock, or water

1 cup mini shell pasta

⅔ cup grated Cheddar cheese

Tip

★ If freezing, freeze the sauce separately, before you mix it with the pasta.

This delicious tomato sauce is enriched with vegetables. It is very versatile; you can mix it with pasta, as here, or combine it with cooked fish or chicken.

Heat the oil in a saucepan, add the onion, and sauté for about 4 minutes until softened. Add the garlic and sauté for a minute, then stir in the sweet potato and carrot, followed by the chopped tomatoes and vegetable stock or water. Bring to a boil, stirring frequently, then cover the pan with a lid and simmer for about 30 minutes until the vegetables are tender.

Meanwhile, cook the pasta according to the package instructions, then drain.

Once cooked, allow the sauce to cool slightly, then blend to a puree in a food processor, or in the saucepan with a hand-held stick blender, then stir in the cheese until melted. Mix the drained pasta with the sauce and serve.

I like to serve this with the Salmon, Quinoa, and Spinach Balls (see page 158) or Salmon Rissoles (see page 160).

Mushroom and Spinach Pasta

⅔ cup mini pasta shells
2 teaspoons butter
⅓ cup finely diced onion
½ cup finely diced chestnut
    mushrooms
1 garlic clove, crushed
1 tablespoon plus 1 teaspoon
    all-purpose flour
1 cup whole milk
¼ teaspoon chopped fresh thyme
⅓ cup grated Parmesan cheese
½ cup finely chopped baby
    spinach

Mini pasta shells or orzo are the perfect size to encourage little ones to chew. Mushrooms provide vitamin B, vitamin D, fiber, and essential minerals like potassium—finely chopping them gives them a more appealing texture for babies.

Cook the pasta according to the package instructions, then drain.

Melt the butter in a saucepan, add the onion, cover with a lid, and sauté for 4 minutes, stirring every now and then, until softened. Add the mushrooms and fry for 3 minutes. Add the garlic and fry for 2 minutes more. Add the flour and cook for 1 minute, then gradually add the milk, stirring for 1–2 minutes until thickened. Remove the pan from the heat, add the thyme, Parmesan, and spinach, and stir until wilted. Stir in the drained pasta and serve.

Baby Vegetable Pasta

MAKES 4 CHILD PORTIONS

½ cup mini shell pasta
2 teaspoons butter
⅓ cup finely chopped onion
¼ cup finely diced peeled carrot
¼ cup seeded and finely diced
    sweet red bell pepper
¼ cup frozen sweet corn
¼ cup frozen peas
1 tablespoon plus 1 teaspoon
    all-purpose flour
1 cup hot unsalted or diluted
    vegetable stock
2 tablespoons chopped fresh basil
1 teaspoon lemon juice
⅓ cup grated Parmesan cheese

As your baby gets older it is important to encourage him to chew, so dice vegetables instead of pureeing them. Frozen peas and sweet corn are always a good standby to keep in your freezer.

● ●

Cook the pasta according to the package instructions, then drain.

Melt the butter in a saucepan. Add the onion, carrot, and pepper, cover with a lid, and sauté for 10 minutes until nearly soft. Then add the sweet corn and peas and sauté for 2 minutes more. Add the flour, cook for 1 minute, then gradually add the stock, stirring until thickened. Simmer for 3 minutes, then stir in the basil, lemon juice, and Parmesan.

Stir in the drained pasta and serve.

Macaroni Cheese ❄

MAKES 4–5 CHILD PORTIONS
1½ cups macaroni pasta
2½ cups whole milk
3 tablespoons cornstarch
¾ cup grated aged
    Cheddar cheese
¾ cup grated Gruyère cheese
½ cup grated Parmesan cheese
½ cup mascarpone
¼ teaspoon Dijon mustard
a little salt and pepper (for
    babies over 12 months old)

Topping
¼ cup dried or ½ cup fresh
    breadcrumbs
4 tablespoons grated Parmesan
    cheese

This is my best-ever macaroni recipe made with three cheeses. Every generation will love this classic dish.

• •

Cook the macaroni according to the package instructions, then drain and rinse under cold running water. Heat 2 cups of the milk in a saucepan until it just reaches boiling point.

Mix the cornstarch and the remaining milk together then whisk the mixture into the hot milk. Cook, whisking constantly, for about 2 minutes, until the sauce thickens and comes to a boil.

Remove from the heat and whisk in the grated cheeses until melted, followed by the mascarpone and Dijon mustard.

Stir in the cooked pasta and season to taste with salt and pepper (if using). Transfer to a baking dish. Mix together the breadcrumbs and Parmesan cheese and sprinkle them over the top and place under the broiler until golden and bubbling.

Remove from the broiler and serve with steamed vegetables, such as broccoli florets.

Poultry

Crispy Chicken Nuggets

MAKES 2–3 CHILD PORTIONS

2 tablespoons sunflower oil

1½ cups crispy rice cereal

1 tablespoon finely grated
   aged Cheddar cheese

1 tablespoon grated
   Parmesan cheese

1 egg

1 tablespoon milk

4 tablespoons all-purpose flour

7 oz (200 g) skinless, boneless
   chicken breast, cut into ½ in
   (1.5 cm) cubes

dips, to serve (optional)

a little salt and pepper (for
   babies over 12 months old)

Tip

★ Alternatively, you can fry the chicken nuggets instead of baking them. Put 3–4 tablespoons of sunflower oil in a large skillet over a medium heat. Fry the nuggets for 2–3 minutes each side, until golden and crisp. Drain on paper towels and cool slightly before serving.

It will be hard to go back to store-bought chicken nuggets after you have tasted these.

Preheat the oven to 400°F (200°C).

Place half the oil in the bowl of a food processor with the crispy rice cereal and grated cheeses, and process to evenly combine (you may need to stop and scrape the mixture down from the sides of the bowl a couple of times). Alternatively, crush the cereal in a plastic baggie with a rolling pin. Transfer the cereal mixture to a wide, shallow bowl or a large plate. Whisk the egg in a small bowl with the milk and mix the flour with a little salt and pepper (if using) and spread it out on a large plate. Grease a baking sheet with the remaining oil.

Toss the chicken cubes in the flour, dip them in the egg, then coat them in the cereal. Place them on the baking sheet and bake for 15 minutes, or until cooked through and crispy, turning after 7 minutes. Serve immediately, with dips if you wish (mayonnaise, ketchup, or one of my dip recipes on page 41).

Sweet Dijon Chicken Kebabs

DAIRY FREE

MAKES 4 KEBABS

1 tablespoon honey or
  maple syrup
½ teaspoon Dijon mustard
½ small garlic clove, crushed
1 teaspoon olive oil
½ teaspoon lemon juice
4 chicken mini fillets, about
  4¼ oz (110 g) in weight,
  or 1 small boneless, skinless
  chicken breast, cubed

You will also need: 4 wooden
  skewers, soaked in warm
  water for 30 minutes

I love honey mustard, and this was the inspiration for the marinade. You can use wholegrain mustard instead, if your children like spicier foods, but I find it has a little too much heat for smaller children. Use maple syrup instead of honey if serving to babies under 12 months.

Combine the honey or maple syrup, mustard, garlic, olive oil, and lemon juice in a small mixing bowl. Add the chicken and toss to coat, then cover the bowl with plastic wrap and refrigerate overnight.

Preheat the broiler to high and line a broiler pan or baking sheet with foil. Remove the chicken from the marinade and thread each piece onto a skewer. Lay the skewers on the foil and spoon over any marinade left in the bowl. Place under the broiler for 3–4 minutes on each side, until the chicken has cooked through.

Remove and allow to cool slightly before serving. Make sure you remove the skewers for smaller children. Serve with cooked rice and steamed vegetables, such as broccoli florets.

Chicken and Kale Balls DAIRY FREE ❄

MAKES 25 BALLS
(ABOUT 5 CHILD PORTIONS)

¾ cup trimmed kale
2 cups fresh breadcrumbs
1 lb 1 oz (500 g) skinless, boneless
   chicken thighs, chopped
1 cup grated carrot
1½ teaspoons grated fresh ginger
1 tablespoon sweet chili sauce
1 teaspoon Chinese five spice
1 teaspoon soy sauce
4 tablespoons all-purpose flour
3 tablespoons canola,
   sunflower, or light olive oil

Tip

★ To make your own fresh
breadcrumbs, process some stale
bread in a food processor.
You can store the breadcrumbs
in a sealed baggie in the freezer—
they are great to have on hand
for coating goujons or arancini.

When my son Nicholas was little and very fussy,
my solution to encourage him to eat chicken was
to process it in a food processor with other
ingredients such as apple and form it into mini
chicken balls. This is a twist on my signature
Chicken and Apple Balls recipe in my *New Complete
Baby & Toddler Meal Planner*, but this time using
carrot and kale and adding some oriental flavors.

• •

Cook the kale in a saucepan of boiling water for 4
minutes, then drain and refresh under cold running
water. Squeeze out the water and finely chop the kale.

Place the chicken thighs in the bowl of a food
processor with the breadcrumbs and process until
roughly chopped (you don't want it too fine).

Transfer to a bowl, add the chopped kale and the
remaining ingredients, and stir to combine. Shape
the mixture into 25 equal-sized balls.

Place the flour on a large plate and roll each ball in
the flour. Heat the oil in a deep-sided skillet and fry
the balls for 8–10 minutes (in 2–3 batches) until golden
and cooked through.

Spiralized Zucchini with Pesto, Tomato, Basil, and Chicken

MAKES 4 CHILD PORTIONS

3 tablespoons olive oil

4 scallions, finely sliced

2 garlic cloves, crushed

4 large tomatoes, skinned, seeded, and roughly chopped

2 tablespoons fresh green pesto

1 cup finely diced cooked chicken breast

1 tablespoon chopped fresh basil leaves

2–3 large zucchinis

⅓ cup finely grated Parmesan cheese

a little salt and pepper (for babies over 12 months old)

It only takes minutes to transform veggies into spaghetti using a spiralizer. I'm not usually one for kitchen gadgets, however this is one is essential for anyone with a reluctant veggie eater. It's so simple and works with other vegetables too, such as sweet potato and carrot.

• •

To make the sauce, heat 1 tablespoon of the oil in a saucepan, add the scallions, and fry for 2 minutes. Add the garlic and fry for 30 seconds, then add the tomatoes, stir, and simmer for 4 minutes until softened. Season lightly with salt and pepper (if using) and add the pesto, chicken, and basil. Stir gently and simmer for 2 minutes, then remove from the heat.

Make the zucchini using a spiralizer to make long spaghetti shapes.

Heat a large skillet until hot. Add the remaining oil and half the zucchini to the pan. Quickly fry for 2 minutes until just softened, then remove from the heat and add the remaining zucchini. Toss together in a bowl.

Add the sauce and mix thoroughly. Sprinkle with the Parmesan and serve.

Chicken, Cherry Tomato, and Sweet Corn Quesadillas

MAKES 4 QUESADILLAS
(6 CHILD PORTIONS)
2 tablespoons olive oil
1 boneless, skinless chicken
  breast, cut into strips
1 teaspoon honey or maple syrup
1 onion, finely sliced
1 teaspoon chopped fresh
  thyme leaves
½ cup chopped fresh cherry
  tomatoes
¼ cup drained canned sweet corn
1 teaspoon balsamic vinegar
½ cup grated Cheddar cheese
6 small tortilla wraps
yogurt, for drizzling
a pinch of paprika (optional)

Quick to prepare, my quesadillas have instant child (and adult) appeal with a yummy chicken filling sandwiched between tortillas and topped with grated Cheddar cheese. Simply fry them on both sides until the cheese has melted. Use maple syrup instead of honey if serving to babies under 12 months old.

• •

Heat half the oil in a skillet, add the chicken and honey, and fry for 3–4 minutes until golden and cooked through. Remove from the pan and set aside.

Add the remaining oil to the pan. Add the onion and thyme and fry for 5 minutes until soft. Add the tomatoes, sweet corn, balsamic vinegar, and chicken and cook for 2 minutes, then transfer to a bowl.

Wipe the skillet clean. Add one of the wraps to the pan. Spoon a third of the chicken mixture on top, sprinkle with a third of the grated cheese, and place another wrap on top.

Push down and fry for 2 minutes, then flip over and cook for another 2 minutes. Slide onto a plate and slice into wedges.

Repeat with the remaining tortillas and serve the wedges drizzled with yogurt and, if you wish, sprinkled with the paprika.

Chicken Teriyaki Sausages

DAIRY FREE

MAKES 25 CHICKEN SAUSAGES

1 onion, chopped

14 oz (400 g) skinless, boneless
    chicken thighs, diced

1 cup grated peeled carrots

1 garlic clove, crushed

2 tablespoons soy sauce

1 teaspoon honey or maple syrup

½ cup dried breadcrumbs, plus
    extra for coating

2–3 tablespoons canola
    or sunflower oil

Yogurt Dip

6 tablespoons plain yogurt

1 teaspoon snipped chives
    or chopped flat-leaf parlsey

¼ cucumber, seeded and coarsely
    grated

Here's how to make your own super-succulent sausages. The addition of soy sauce makes them extra crave-worthy! Use plenty of brown meat from the chicken as this contains more iron than the white breast meat. Use maple syrup instead of honey if serving to babies under 12 months.

Put the onion in the bowl of a food processor and process until finely chopped. Add the chicken and briefly process again. Add the remaining ingredients and process until everything is finely chopped.

Transfer the mixture to a bowl and shape it into 25 equal-sized sausages. Place some extra breadcrumbs on a plate and roll the sausages in the breadcrumbs to coat.

Heat the oil in a skillet and fry the sausages in 2 batches for about 10 minutes until golden and cooked through.

Combine the ingredients for the dip in a separate bowl and serve with the sausages.

Chicken with Tomatoes and Orzo ⊘ DAIRY FREE ❄

MAKES 4 CHILD PORTIONS

3 tablespoons olive oil
1 red onion, diced
1 sweet red bell pepper, seeded and finely diced
2 garlic cloves, crushed
1 teaspoon sweet smoked paprika
1 teaspoon soft brown sugar
1 teaspoon balsamic vinegar
1 cup orzo pasta
2 cups hot unsalted or diluted chicken stock
1 cup passata or tomato sauce
1 teaspoon chopped fresh thyme
10 cherry tomatoes, quartered
2 boneless, skinless chicken breasts, cut into strips, or 2 pre-cooked chicken breasts
a little salt and pepper (for babies over 12 months old)
a handful of basil leaves (optional)

Is it pasta? Is it rice? If you haven't used orzo before it looks like rice but it is in fact pasta and has a soft texture which is perfect for little ones. Sweet smoked paprika, balsamic vinegar, and fresh thyme make this a tasty meal for the whole family.

• •

Heat 1 tablespoon of the oil in a deep skillet, add the onion and pepper, and fry for 3–4 minutes.

Add the garlic and paprika, and fry for 30 seconds, then add the sugar, balsamic vinegar, and orzo. Stir to coat the pasta in the mixture, then add the stock and passata or tomato sauce. Bring to a boil, cover, lower heat, and simmer for 15–20 minutes, until the pasta is cooked and most of the liquid has been absorbed. Add the thyme and tomatoes and stir until the tomatoes have softened.

Season the chicken strips with salt and pepper (if using) and fry them in the remaining oil until lightly golden and cooked through. Alternatively add the cooked chicken cut into strips and heat through. Add them to the pasta and serve with steamed broccoli florets and baby carrots. Chop the basil leaves and add with the chicken (if using).

Broccoli, Chicken, and Potato Bites ❄

MAKES 8 BITES

⅔ cup broccoli florets
¾ cup cold cooked mashed potato
¼ cup grated Parmesan cheese
½ cup diced cooked chicken
⅓ cup dried breadcrumbs
1 egg, beaten
2 scallions, finely sliced
2 tablespoons canola or
   sunflower oil
a little salt and pepper (for
   babies over 12 months old)

These bites have been very popular on my Instagram. They have received comments like, "Never mind the kids, I want to eat these up!" They are so easy to make and you can freeze them when cooked and cooled, simply reheating in the oven when needed. This is also a great leftover recipe, for those days when you have cooked meat left over from a roast (see my Roast Chicken on page 126).

• •

Steam the broccoli florets for 5–6 minutes until tender, then set aside until they are completely cool. Once cool, chop them finely.

Mix together the cold mashed potato, chopped broccoli, grated cheese, chicken, half the breadcrumbs, half the beaten egg, and the scallions. Season with salt and pepper (if using).

Shape the mixture into 8 sausage shapes, then coat them in the remaining egg and roll them in the remaining breadcrumbs. Transfer to a lined plate or baking sheet and refrigerate for 30 minutes.

Heat the oil in a skillet. Fry until golden and heated through. Serve with ketchup or a dip of your choice (see my dips on page 41).

Griddled Chicken with Three Quick Sauces

2 skinless, boneless chicken breasts
1 tablespoon olive or sunflower oil
1 garlic clove, peeled and halved
a little salt and pepper

Three Quick Sauces

MILD CURRY
2 tablespoons mayonnaise
2 tablespoons Greek-style yogurt
1½ teaspoons mild curry paste
1 teaspoon honey
2–3 drops of lemon juice

EASY BARBECUE
3 tablespoons ketchup
1 tablespoon honey
¼ teaspoon soy sauce
¼ teaspoon lemon juice
2 teaspoons water

SPICY TOMATO
3 tablespoons ketchup
1 tablespoon sweet chili sauce
1 tablespoon water
¼ teaspoon soy sauce

Chicken without a breadcrumb or batter coating can still be super tasty. Simply marinate it and cook it on a grill pan, griddle, or in a skillet, and serve it with one of these three delicious sauces.

• •

Cover the chicken breasts with plastic wrap and bash with a mallet or rolling pin to flatten.

Brush the fillets with oil, then rub one of the cut sides of the garlic clove over them. Season with a little salt and pepper.

Brush a grill pan with oil and when it is very hot cook the chicken on one side for 2–3 minutes, then turn the heat down a little and cook for another 3 minutes. Turn the chicken breasts over and repeat on the other side, until cooked through.

Cut the chicken into strips and follow one of the quick sauce recipes to make tasty dipping sauces for the chicken. Serve with steamed vegetables, such as garden peas, sugar snap peas, baby carrots, and broccoli florets.

For the Three Quick Sauces: Mix all the ingredients together for your sauce of choice and serve with the griddled chicken.

Cherub's Chicken Couscous

MAKES 4 CHILD PORTIONS

1 cup unsalted or diluted
　chicken stock
Scant ½ cup couscous
1 tablespoon unsalted butter
½ small onion, finely chopped
⅓ cup diced zucchini
½ garlic clove, crushed
2 plum tomatoes, seeded
　and chopped
½ cup diced cooked chicken
1 tablespoon chopped basil
1 tablespoon grated Parmesan
　cheese
　a little salt and pepper (for
　babies over 12 months old)

Couscous has a soft texture which makes it perfect for babies who are lacking in teeth, although you'll be surprised what gums can get through! I love to add fresh herbs to baby food to maximize flavor, and here I've used basil.

•·•

Bring the stock to the boil in a saucepan. Put the couscous in a heatproof bowl. Pour over the hot stock, stir, and cover with plastic wrap. Set aside for 15 minutes to absorb the liquid.

Meanwhile, melt the butter in a saucepan, add the onion, and sauté for 2 minutes, then add the diced zucchini and garlic and sauté for 3 minutes more. Add the tomatoes and cook for 1 minute, and finally add the chicken and basil.

Stir the chicken mixture into the couscous, season lightly with salt and pepper (if using), then add the Parmesan and mix gently before serving.

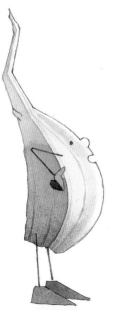

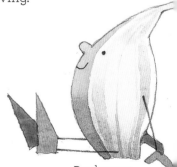

Roast Chicken with Vegetables and Gravy

DAIRY FREE

MAKES 5 ADULT PORTIONS
OR 10 CHILD PORTIONS

1 x 3 lb 3 oz (1.5 kg) organic
　　chicken
1 tablespoon chopped
　　fresh rosemary
3 garlic cloves, crushed
2 tablespoons olive oil
1 tablespoon honey
　　(or maple syrup, if serving
　　to babies under 12 months old)
a little salt and pepper (for
　　babies over 12 months old)

Roast Vegetables
1 lb 8 oz (800 g) white potatoes,
　　peeled and cut into large pieces
6 tablespoons sunflower oil
3 parsnips, peeled and sliced
　　into batons
1 lb 1 oz (500 g) baby carrots

Gravy
3 tablespoons all-purpose flour
Scant 2 cups hot chicken stock
Worcestershire sauce to taste

Making one meal for the whole family not only saves time, but it encourages everyone to eat together, which I love. Here is my favorite roast chicken recipe, which is also suitable for sharing with your baby. I have come up with five different delicious and baby-friendly ways to use up the leftover roast chicken, which follow on from this recipe.

• •

Preheat the oven to 350°F (180°C).

Put the chicken in a roasting pan.

Mix the rosemary, garlic, and oil together in a bowl. Pour over the chicken and season with salt and pepper (if using). Roast for 1¼ hours until golden brown and cooked through. To test if it's ready, push a sharp knife into the thickest part of one of the thighs, and if the juices run clear, it's done.

Put the potatoes in a saucepan, cover with cold salted water, bring to a boil, and cook for 5 minutes. Drain thoroughly. Drizzle 4 tablespoons of the oil into a roasting pan and heat it in the oven. Once it's hot, add the potatoes and coat them in the oil. Roast for 30–40 minutes, turning them once, until golden and crispy.

Put the parsnips and carrots in a large roasting pan.

Drizzle over the remaining oil and season with salt and pepper (if using). Roast for 30 minutes, tossing them halfway through the cooking time, until golden and cooked through.

Drizzle the honey or maple syrup over the chicken 15 minutes before the end of the cooking time.

Transfer the chicken to a large serving plate, cover loosely with foil, and leave it to rest while you make the gravy.

To make the gravy, skim 3 tablespoons of fat off the cooking juices. Add the flour to the roasting pan and whisk it over the heat for 1 minute. Whisk in the stock, Worcestershire sauce, and chicken juices, and cook, stirring, until thickened and bubbling.

Serve the roast chicken, gravy, and roast vegetables with steamed broccoli.

Chicken Corn Soup

MAKES 6 CHILD PORTIONS
1 tablespoon sunflower oil
1 onion, finely chopped
1 teaspoon grated fresh ginger
2 garlic cloves, sliced
1 cup drained canned sweet corn
2¾ cups unsalted or diluted
    chicken stock
1½ tablespoons cornstarch
a pinch of chili flakes (optional)
2 teaspoons soy sauce
5 scallions, thinly sliced
a pinch of sugar
juice of ½ lemon
1 cup finely chopped
    cooked chicken
sesame oil to taste (optional)
a little salt and pepper (for
    babies over 12 months old)

Here's a creamy chicken soup with a Chinese twist. You can set aside your baby's portion before adding the soy sauce.

Heat the oil in a saucepan, add the onion, ginger, and garlic, and fry for 4–5 minutes, then add the sweet corn and stir over the heat for 30 seconds.

Add the chicken stock, cover, and simmer for 5–8 minutes, then remove from the heat and blend until smooth with a hand-held stick blender.

Mix the cornstarch with a little cold water and add it to the soup, then cook over a medium heat, stirring, until thickened.

Add the remaining ingredients to the soup. Season with salt and pepper (if using) and simmer for 1 minute until the chicken is heated through. Serve with fresh bread.

Chicken Curry

DAIRY FREE ❄

MAKES 2 CHILD PORTIONS

1 teaspoon canola or
   sunflower oil
½ cup chopped onion
½ cup grated apple
1 garlic clove, crushed
1 teaspoon mild curry paste
2 teaspoons all-purpose flour
1¼ cups hot unsalted
   or diluted chicken stock
1 teaspoon soy sauce
1 teaspoon mango chutney
¾ cup diced cooked chicken
cooked rice, to serve

Here is a flavorsome chicken curry that the whole family will love (scale it up to make enough for the grown-ups, too).

• •

Heat the oil in a saucepan, add the onion, apple, and garlic, and fry for 2–3 minutes, then add the mild curry paste and flour, and stir over the heat for 1 minute. Stir in the stock, soy sauce, and mango chutney. Bring to a boil, cover, and simmer for 5–8 minutes.

Remove from the heat and blend to the desired consistency using a hand-held stick blender, then stir in the chicken and serve with cooked rice and steamed vegetables.

Chicken and Sweet Corn Croquettes ❄

MAKES 20 CROQUETTES

2 cups fresh breadcrumbs
5 scallions, roughly chopped
1 cup grated peeled carrots
¼ cup drained canned sweet corn
¼ cup fresh basil leaves
⅞ cup diced cooked chicken
1–2 tablespoons sweet chili sauce
½ cup grated aged
    Cheddar cheese
1 egg yolk
2 tablespoons all-purpose flour,
    plus extra for coating
2 tablespoons sunflower oil
a little salt and pepper (for
    babies over 12 months old)

Leftover Roast Chicken

Spice up your child's dinner time and use up all those leftovers with these tasty and nourishing croquettes. Once cooked, you can freeze the croquettes in a plastic container, separated by wax or parchment paper. Reheat in a microwave from frozen or in an oven preheated to 350°F (180°C) for about 15 minutes or until hot throughout.

Place the breadcrumbs, scallions, carrot, sweet corn, basil, and chicken in a food processor and process until finely chopped. Add the sweet chili sauce, cheese, egg yolk, and flour. Process again for 2 seconds. Season with salt and pepper (if using).

Transfer the mixture to a mixing bowl, then shape into 20 equal-sized croquettes. Place some extra flour on a plate or cutting board and roll the croquettes in the flour. Transfer to a baking sheet and chill in the refrigerator for at least 10 minutes (or up to 24 hours before you are ready to cook them).

When ready to serve, heat the oil in a skillet. Fry the croquettes for 3–4 minutes (in 2 batches) until golden all over. Transfer to a plate lined with paper towels. Leave for a few minutes to firm up before serving with roasted vegetables, such as sweet potato wedges, and some steamed vegetables.

Little Chicken and Leek Pies ❄

MAKES 4 CHILD PORTIONS

1 cup diced peeled potatoes

1 cup diced peeled carrots

1 tablespoon plus 1 teaspoon
butter

2 small leeks, trimmed and
roughly chopped

2 skinless, boneless chicken
breasts, cut into ¾ in (2 cm)
cubes

3 mushrooms, thinly sliced

2 tablespoons all-purpose flour

1 cup whole milk

½ cup grated Cheddar cheese

⅛ cup drained canned sweet corn

a little salt and pepper (for
babies over 12 months old)

Leftover Roast Chicken

Individual pots are the perfect size for your little one and look so much more child-friendly than serving small portions on a big plate.

Put the potatoes and carrots in a saucepan of water, bring to a boil, and simmer for 10–12 minutes until soft. Drain, then mash until smooth.

Melt the butter in a saucepan. Add the leeks and sauté for 5 minutes, until just soft, then add the chicken and fry for 2 minutes. Next, add the mushrooms and cook for 2 minutes. Sprinkle over the flour, stir for 1 minute, then gradually stir in the milk and bring to a boil. Simmer gently for 5 minutes, until the chicken is cooked. While it's simmering, preheat the broiler.

Add three-quarters of the grated cheese to the sauce, season with salt and pepper (if using), and add the sweet corn. Divide the mixture between the 4 individual pots. Spoon the mashed potato and carrot on top, and sprinkle with the remaining cheese.

Place under the broiler for 4–5 minutes, until lightly golden on top and bubbling around the edges. Serve with peas.

Fish

Monkfish Kebabs

DAIRY FREE

MAKES 4 KEBABS

1 lb 1 oz (500 g) monkfish fillets

4 tablespoons olive oil

1 teaspoon chopped fresh thyme

juice of ½ lemon

a pinch of finely diced red
   chili (optional)

½ small garlic clove, crushed

1 small zucchini, cut into
   ¼ in- (0.5 cm-) thick rounds

You will also need: 4 wooden
   skewers, soaked in warm
   water for 30 minutes

A slightly more robust and firm-fleshed fish, monkfish is a good option to serve for hand-eating toddlers. I recommend omitting the chili for babies.

• •

Remove the monkfish fillets from the bone, trim away any membrane, and cut the fish into bite-sized pieces.

Combine half the oil with the thyme, lemon juice, chili, and garlic in a bowl. Add the fish pieces, coat them in the marinade, then set aside for 5 minutes.

Thread the zucchini and marinated monkfish pieces onto the soaked skewers.

Heat a deep-sided skillet until hot and fry the kebabs in the remaining oil for 2–3 minutes on each side until golden and cooked through. Remove from the heat and let cool slightly before serving. Remove the skewers before giving to young children.

Fish Chowder ❄

MAKES 6 CHILD PORTIONS
2 teaspoons sunflower oil
1 cup chopped trimmed leeks
⅞ cup diced carrots
1½ cups diced peeled potatoes
⅞ cup unsalted
   or diluted fish stock
⅔ cup whole milk

I love this deconstructed fish pie. The tender cubes of fish and vegetables mingle in a light cheesy sauce flavored with fresh dill.

• •

Heat the oil in a saucepan. Add the leek and carrots and stir over a medium heat for 2 minutes, then cover with a lid and cook gently for 5 minutes until soft.

9 oz (250 g) mixed skinless
   and boneless cod and salmon
   (or just white fish), diced
⅜ cup frozen peas
1 tablespoon chopped fresh dill
2 tablespoons grated Parmesan

Remove the lid and add the potatoes and stock. Bring to a boil, cover, and simmer for 10–12 minutes, until the potatoes are cooked through, then add the milk, fish, and peas. Simmer for 5 minutes until the fish is cooked through. Remove from the heat, stir in the dill and Parmesan, and serve.

Salmon Fishcakes ❄

MAKES 18–20 MINI FISHCAKES

1 large (9 oz/250 g) potato
2 tablespoons mayonnaise
1½ tablespoons sweet chili sauce
1 teaspoon lemon juice
4 scallions, finely sliced
⅜ cup grated Cheddar cheese
2 tablespoons ketchup
9 oz (250 g) skinless, boneless
    salmon, cut into small cubes
2 teaspoons chopped fresh dill
2 cups fresh breadcrumbs
3–4 tablespoons sunflower oil
    for frying
a little salt and pepper (for
    babies over 12 months old)

These deliciously moist salmon fishcakes are flavored with a little sweet chili sauce, Cheddar cheese, and fresh dill. You can keep the breadcrumb-coated (but uncooked) fishcakes in the refrigerator overnight if you don't want to cook them all on the same day, or else freeze them for cooking later.

• •

Prick the potato with a fork and microwave on high for 10 minutes until soft, or bake in a 400°F (200°C) oven for 1 hour, or until soft. As soon as the potato is cool enough on handle, cut in half, scoop out the fluffy potato into a bowl, and mash it with a fork. Allow to cool for a few minutes.

Add the mayonnaise, sweet chili sauce, lemon juice, scallion, grated cheese, and ketchup to the mashed potato and roughly combine.

Stir in the cubes of salmon, dill, and half the breadcrumbs, and season lightly with salt and pepper (if using).

Using your hands, form the mixture into about 8 fishcakes. Tip the remaining breadcrumbs onto a large plate and coat the fishcakes in the crumbs.

Heat the oil in a large skillet and fry the fishcakes for about 5 minutes on each side until golden. Drain on paper towels, then serve.

Salmon and Cod Fish Pie ❋

MAKES 6 CHILD PORTIONS

1 cup diced peeled carrots

4 cups diced peeled potatoes

3 tablespoons butter, plus a knob for the mash

1 large onion, finely chopped

⅓ cup all-purpose flour

1⅔ cups whole milk, plus 2 tablespoons for the mash

1 teaspoon Dijon mustard

2 teaspoons lemon juice

1½ teaspoons rice wine vinegar

½ cup grated Cheddar cheese

¼ cup grated Parmesan cheese

1½ tablespoons chopped fresh dill

7 oz (200 g) boneless, skinless salmon fillet, cubed

7 oz (200g) boneless, skinless cod fillet, cubed

1 egg, lightly beaten

You can make small portions of fish pie for your little ones, but I've met plenty of moms and dads who proudly serve it for adult dinners. The fish, added just before it is baked with the topping, stays moist throughout the cooking process. Oily fish such as salmon is a great source of omega-3 oils, which are very important for your baby's brain and visual development. Here, the veggie content is given a boost with a tasty mashed carrot and potato topping.

Preheat the oven to 400°F (200°C).

Boil the carrots in a pan of water for 8 minutes, then add the diced potatoes and boil for 12–15 minutes more until soft. Drain, mash, and mix with 2 tablespoons of butter and the 2 tablespoons of milk.

Melt the rest of the butter in a pan, add the onion, and sauté for 5–6 minutes until soft. Add the flour, stir over the heat for a minute, then gradually whisk in the milk. Add the Dijon mustard, lemon juice, and vinegar, and stir for a few minutes over a low heat until thick. Remove from the heat and add both the cheeses, dill, and fish. Spoon the mixture into an ovenproof dish and spoon the mashed potato and carrot on top. Brush the top with the beaten egg and bake for 30 minutes until bubbling and golden on top. Serve with peas.

Crispy Fish Fingers

1½ cups crispy rice cereal

3 tablespoons grated
    Parmesan cheese

¼ teaspoon paprika

1 egg

2 tablespoons all-purpose flour

8 oz (225 g) skinless, boneless
    white fish fillets, cut into little
    finger-sized strips

2–3 tablespoons sunflower oil

a little salt and pepper (for
    babies over 12 months old)

Dip

2 tablespoons mayonnaise

2 tablespoons Greek-style yogurt

1 teaspoon fresh lemon juice

a pinch of salt (optional)

Tip

★ To freeze, place the coated but uncooked pieces of fish on a lined baking sheet and freeze uncovered. When frozen, transfer to a plastic freezer container.

Crispy rice cereal makes a tasty, crunchy coating for fish. These goujons cook quickly and can be cooked from frozen. Crushed cornflakes also make a good alternative coating: coat the fish in flour and egg, as instructed below, then roll them in cornflakes.

Put the crispy rice cereal, Parmesan, and paprika in the bowl of a food processor and process to form fine crumbs. Transfer to a large plate and stir in salt and pepper (if using). Beat the egg in a bowl with a pinch of salt (if using). Place the flour on a separate plate.

Toss 3–4 fish pieces in the flour, dip them in the egg, then coat them in the cereal coating. Place the coated fish pieces on a clean plate and continue with remaining fish. Cook immediately or freeze (see Tip).

Heat the oil in a large skillet and fry the fish fingers for 1½–2 minutes on each side, until golden and cooked through. Transfer to a paper towel-lined plate to cool slightly before serving.

Alternatively, place the fish fingers on a greased non-stick baking sheet, drizzle with a little oil, and bake for 12 minutes in an oven preheated to 400°F (200°C).

To make the dip, combine the ingredients in a bowl and season with salt (if you wish). Serve the fish fingers with the dip and some peas.

Tuna and Orzo Pasta

MAKES 3 CHILD PORTIONS

1 tablespoon olive oil

1 onion, chopped

½ sweet red bell pepper, seeded and diced

½ garlic clove, crushed

½ x 14.5 oz (411 g) can chopped tomatoes

½ cup unsalted or diluted vegetable stock

¼ cup drained canned tuna in oil

⅛ cup drained canned sweet corn

½ cup orzo pasta

Here's a quick and easy recipe that you can have on the table in 20 minutes. Orzo pasta is good for introducing babies to texture as it resembles small grains of rice, but you could substitute any mini pasta shape.

• •

Heat the oil in a saucepan, Add the onion and bell pepper and fry for 5 minutes, then add the garlic and fry for 30 seconds.

Add the chopped tomatoes and stock and simmer for 15 minutes, then add the tuna and sweet corn.

Cook the orzo according to the package instructions until just firm. Drain and mix with the sauce, then serve.

Tuna Muffin Melts

MAKES 2 CHILD PORTIONS
¾ cup drained canned tuna in oil
1 scallion, finely chopped
2 tablespoons Greek-style yogurt
2 tablespoons tomato ketchup
¼ teaspoon lemon juice
2 dashes of Worcestershire sauce
   (optional)
2 English muffins, split in half
⅜ cup grated Cheddar cheese
a little salt and pepper (for
   babies over 12 months old)

Halved, toasted English muffins are an ideal size for smaller children to pick up and eat. If you have more tuna melt filling than you need, don't worry—it will stay fresh, covered, in the refrigerator for 2–3 days and makes a great sandwich or quesadilla filling.

• •

Preheat the broiler to high.

Put the tuna and scallion in a bowl and stir in the yogurt, ketchup, lemon juice, and Worcestershire sauce (if using). Season to taste with salt and pepper (if using).

Lightly toast the English muffin halves, then pile the tuna mix onto the four cut sides. Scatter over the grated cheese and place under the broiler for 1–2 minutes, until the cheese has melted. Cool slightly, then serve cut in half or into quarters. Serve with salad, or hummus or avocado dip with breadsticks or crudités.

Variation: Tuna Quesadilla

Spread half of the tuna mix over a wheat tortilla wrap, scatter over 4 tablespoons grated cheese, then top with a second wrap; dry-fry or broil for around 2 minutes on each side, until crisp.

Bow-Tie Pasta Salad with Tuna

DAIRY FREE

MAKES 4 CHILD PORTIONS

Salad

1½ cups pasta bows

1 shallot, finely chopped

⅞ cup drained and flaked canned tuna in oil

4 cherry tomatoes

¼ cup cooked frozen or canned sweet corn

1 small avocado, halved, pitted, peeled, and cut into small cubes

Dressing

2 tablespoons mayonnaise

2 tablespoons olive oil

2 teaspoons lemon juice

a pinch of cayenne pepper (optional)

Bow-tie pasta is an easy shape for little ones to pick up. Lots of babies and toddlers love it with a little melted butter and grated Parmesan. Alternatively, you can make into a delicious tuna salad, leaving out the cayenne pepper for young babies.

Cook the pasta bows according to the package instructions.

Mix together all the ingredients for the salad in a bowl (except the avocado—add this just before serving or it will discolor).

Combine the dressing ingredients. Drain the pasta, allow to cool, then mix with the salad. Add the avocado and toss in the dressing.

Mini Baked Potatoes with Tuna and Corn

MAKES 3 CHILD PORTIONS

6 large new potatoes
⅜ cup drained canned tuna
2 tablespoons drained canned
    sweet corn
2 tablespoons mayonnaise
4 cherry tomatoes, quartered
1 tablespoon grated Cheddar
    cheese

This easy recipe makes the perfect standby meal, because it uses budget-friendly ingredients that are staple foods in most households.

• •

Preheat the oven to 400°F (200°C).

Prick the potatoes and place them on a baking sheet. Bake in the oven for 30–35 minutes; alternatively, prick the potatoes and microwave for 7–10 minutes until soft.

As soon as they are cool enough on handle, slice in half vertically, but not all the way through. Mix the drained tuna, sweet corn, mayonnaise, tomatoes, and cheese together and spoon the mixture equally onto each baked potato.

Tuna Tortilla Tartlets ❄

MAKES 12 TUNA TARTLETS
a little sunflower oil for greasing
3 mini tortilla wraps
⅛ cup drained canned tuna in oil
⅛ cup drained canned sweet corn
3 cherry tomatoes, quartered
1 egg
3 tablespoons sour cream
2 tablespoons finely grated
   Parmesan cheese
a little mustard cress, to garnish
a little salt and pepper (for
   babies over 12 months old)

Transform tortillas into these tasty tartlets by cutting them into circles using a cookie cutter and pressing them into a mini muffin pan.

Preheat the oven to 350°F (180°C) and grease a 12-hole mini muffin pan with oil.

Stamp out 12 x 3-inch (7-cm) circles from the 3 wraps.

Push the tortilla discs into the muffin pan holes to make 12 little tortilla liners. Divide the tuna, sweet corn, and tomatoes between the liners.

Mix the egg and sour cream together in a small mixing bowl, season lightly with salt and pepper (if using), and divide it equally between the liners. Sprinkle with the cheese. Bake for 15–18 minutes until golden on top and set in the middle. Remove from the oven, sprinkle with cress, and serve with carrot and cucumber sticks, and sugar snap peas.

Tuna and Broccoli Pasta

MAKES 8 CHILD PORTIONS

2½ cups mini shell pasta
⅞ cup broccoli florets
3 tablespoons butter
⅓ cup all-purpose flour
3 cups whole milk, warmed
2 teaspoons Dijon mustard
½ cup grated Cheddar cheese
⅓ cup grated Parmesan cheese
¾ cup drained canned tuna in oil
½ cup quartered cherry tomatoes

Those little green trees which little ones often love to hate make a great finger food. Try this recipe and they'll soon be eating entire forests!

• •

Cook the pasta according to the package instructions. Add the broccoli florets 3 minutes before the end of the cooking time. Reserve 3 tablespoons of the pasta cooking water before draining.

Melt the butter in a saucepan, add the flour, and stir over the heat for a minute, then gradually whisk in the milk, stirring until thickened. Add the mustard and grated cheeses. Remove from the heat and add the cooked pasta, broccoli, tuna, and tomatoes, plus the reserved pasta cooking water, and stir together.

Serve with raw vegetables and a dip, if you wish.

★ For a smooth white sauce, always heat the milk before stirring it into the flour and butter.

Cod with Herb Butter

MAKES 8 CHILD PORTIONS

2 tablespoons softened butter
2 tablespoons chopped fresh
   mixed herbs, e.g. parsley,
   thyme, oregano
1 tablespoon lemon juice
1 lb (450 g) thick skinless,
   boneless cod fillets
a little salt and pepper (for
   babies over 12 months old)

Give white fish a lift with a squeeze of lemon, fresh herbs, and butter. You can also make this recipe with any other firm white fish, such as haddock, halibut, or pollock.

Preheat the oven to 350°F (180°C).

Mix the softened butter with the chopped herbs and lemon juice. Place the fish in a small ovenproof dish, season with salt and pepper (if using), and spread the herb butter over the top.

Transfer to the oven and bake for 8–10 minutes until the fish is opaque and cooked through. Remove from the oven and flake the cooked fish with a fork, checking to make sure that there are no bones, and serve it with Parmesan Roasted Sweet Potato Wedges (see page 61).

Salmon, Quinoa, and Spinach Balls ❄

MAKES 20 BALLS

½ cup quinoa

1 sweet potato

1¾ cup fresh white breadcrumbs

6 oz (175 g) skinless, boneless salmon fillet, sliced

1 cup spinach, roughly chopped

⅓ cup grated Parmesan cheese

5 scallions, sliced

1 teaspoon fish sauce

1 tablespoon sweet chili sauce

2 tablespoons all-purpose flour

sunflower oil for frying

a little salt and pepper (for babies over 12 months old)

Dill Sauce

2 teaspoons sunflower oil

1 large leek, trimmed and finely chopped

½ teaspoon white wine vinegar

4 teaspoons all-purpose flour

1¼ cups unsalted or diluted fish stock

½ cup milk

½ teaspoon Dijon mustard

4 tablespoons grated Parmesan cheese

¼ cup half and half

1 teaspoon lemon juice

1 teaspoon fresh chopped dill

We ran a competition to find the cover star for this book. I made a batch of these balls for the finalists' photoshoot and couldn't believe how quickly they were eaten! They are just perfect for little fingers.

• •

Cook the quinoa in a pan of lightly salted boiling water for 15 minutes until tender. Drain, rinse, then leave to drain in a strainer for about 10 minutes.

Prick the sweet potato with a fork and cook it in the microwave for 7–10 minutes or bake at 400°F (200°C) for 45 minutes. Once cool, remove the skin.

To make the dill sauce, sauté the leek in the oil for 4–5 minutes until softened. Stir in the vinegar and cook for 30 seconds, then stir in the flour and cook for 1 minute. Add the fish stock, milk, and mustard, and cook, stirring, for about 5 minutes until thickened. Remove from the heat, stir in the Parmesan until melted, then add the half and half, lemon juice, and dill.

Process the sweet potato in a food processor with the quinoa, breadcrumbs, salmon, spinach, Parmesan, scallions, fish sauce, and chili sauce, and seasoning (if using), until finely chopped.

Shape the mixture into 20 equal-sized balls. Lightly coat the balls in the flour. Heat a little oil in a skillet and fry the balls in batches for 5–6 minutes until golden and cooked through. Serve with the dill sauce.

Salmon Rissoles

MAKES 6 RISSOLES

1 x 7½ oz (215 g) canned red
   salmon in oil, drained
2 tablespoons dried breadcrumbs,
   plus extra for coating
2 tablespoons ketchup
3 scallions, finely chopped
2 tablespoons sunflower oil

A tasty recipe made with just four ingredients. Canned salmon is a good source of calcium, so this is a perfect recipe for babies or toddlers with a cow's milk allergy.

• •

Transfer the canned salmon to a mixing bowl. Add the remaining ingredients (except the oil), flake the salmon with a fork, and mix everything together with a spoon. Shape the mixture into 6 rissoles.

Spread a few tablespoons of breadcrumbs onto a large plate and coat the rissoles in the breadcrumbs.

Heat the oil in a skillet and fry the rissoles for 2–3 minutes, turning them once, until golden and cooked through. Serve with Kale and Veggie Mash (see page 63).

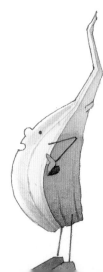

Pasta Shells with Salmon and Veggies in a Light Cheese Sauce ❄

MAKES 6 CHILD PORTIONS

7 oz (200g) skinless,
    boneless salmon fillet
2 tablespoons butter
1½ cups mini shell pasta
⅞ cup broccoli florets
2 tablespoons olive oil
1 large onion, thinly sliced
1 garlic clove, crushed
1¼ cup diced, seeded and peeled
    butternut squash
1 cup unsalted or diluted
    vegetable stock
⅞ cup crème fraîche
1 cup halved cherry tomatoes
    (quartered if large)
½ cup grated Parmesan cheese
a squeeze of lemon juice
a little salt and pepper (for
    babies over 12 months old)

Let me introduce you to my Cheat's Cheese Sauce. It's lighter than a classic roux-based sauce because it is made with vegetable stock.

Preheat the oven to 350°F (180°C).

Put the salmon in the center of a piece of foil, add the butter on top, and season with salt and pepper (if using). Fold the foil over the fish to wrap, place it on a baking sheet, and bake for 15 minutes until cooked through. Remove from the oven, unwrap, and flake the fish into large pieces.

Cook the pasta according to the package instructions, adding the broccoli florets 2 minutes before the end of the cooking time.

While the pasta is cooking, make the sauce. Heat the oil in a deep-sided skillet, add the onion, garlic, and squash, and fry for 5 minutes, then add the stock. Cover and simmer for 5 minutes or until the squash is tender. Remove the lid and stir in the crème fraîche and salmon. Stir in the pasta and broccoli until heated through, then remove from the heat. Add the tomatoes, Parmesan, and lemon juice, and serve.

Sesame-coated Salmon

MAKES 4 CHILD PORTIONS

1 teaspoon grated fresh ginger
1 tablespoon soy sauce
1 tablespoon sweet chili sauce,
    plus extra to serve
2 skinless, boneless salmon fillets,
    cut into bite-sized chunks
    (about 4 chunks per fillet)
1 tablespoon sesame seeds
1¼ cups cooked noodles
wedges of lime, to serve
sweet chili sauce, to serve
    (optional)

Transform salmon in a matter of minutes with this finger-licking marinade. If your child has a gluten or egg allergy, you could use rice noodles instead of egg noodles. Sesame seeds should be safe for your baby from 6 months. However, very occasionally, babies can have a sesame allergy. If your baby has severe eczema, then you may need to be cautious as there is an increased risk of food allergy.

• •

Preheat the oven to 350°F (180°C) and line a baking sheet with parchment paper.

Place the ginger, soy sauce, and sweet chili sauce in a bowl. Add the salmon chunks, coat them in the marinade, and set aside for 10 minutes.

Place the marinated salmon pieces on the lined baking sheet and sprinkle them with the sesame seeds.

Roast for 7 minutes, until lightly golden and cooked through.

Serve with the noodles, wedges of lime, and a small bowl of sweet chili sauce for dipping (if you wish).

Meat

Bolognese Sauce ❄

MAKES 8–10 CHILD PORTIONS

2 tablespoons olive oil

2 onions, finely diced

⅔ cup finely diced peeled carrots

⅔ cup diced zucchini

¼ cup seeded and finely diced
   sweet red bell pepper

⅓ cup diced celery

2 garlic cloves, crushed

2 x 14.5 oz (411 g) cans
   chopped tomatoes

1 tablespoon sun-dried
   tomato paste

2 teaspoons chopped fresh thyme

1 lb 1 oz (500 g) lean ground beef

⅔ cup unsalted or diluted
   beef stock

12 oz (350 g) spaghetti, to serve

grated Parmesan cheese, to serve

1 tablespoon chopped fresh basil,
   to serve

Garlic Bread (optional)

1 small baguette

2 tablespoons softened butter

1 garlic clove, crushed

2 teaspoons chopped
   flat-leaf parsley

It's important to introduce red meat into your baby's diet from 6 months as the iron reserves they are born with start to run out, and red meat, like in this bolognese, provides an easily absorbable source.

• •

Heat half the oil in a saucepan, add the onions, carrots, zucchini, red bell pepper, and celery, and sauté for 5 minutes, then add the garlic and sauté for 30 seconds more. Add the chopped tomatoes, tomato paste, and thyme, bring to a boil, then reduce the heat, cover, and simmer for 20 minutes. Remove from the heat and blend until smooth using a hand-held blender.

Heat the remaining oil in a skillet over a high heat, add the ground beef, and fry it (in batches if necessary) until browned, breaking up any lumps with a wooden spoon. Add the beef to the tomato sauce with the stock. Return the skillet to the heat and simmer for 30 minutes.

Cook the spaghetti according to the package instructions, then drain. Serve the bolognaise with spaghetti, sprinkled with grated Parmesan and basil.

For the garlic bread (if serving), preheat the oven to 350°F (180°C). Cut 6 shallow slices in the baguette. Combine the butter, garlic, and parsley, and spread it into the slits and over the top of the bread. Wrap in foil, place on a baking sheet, and bake for 10 minutes, then unwrap and bake for 5 minutes more.

Bolognese Pasta Bake ❄

MAKES 4–6 CHILD PORTIONS
1½ cups fusilli pasta
½ quantity Bolognese Sauce (see page 166), around 1 lb (450 g)

Cheese Sauce
1 tablespoon plus 1 teaspoon butter
2 tablespoons all-purpose flour
2 cup whole milk, warmed
1 teaspoon Dijon mustard
⅜ cup grated Parmesan cheese

Leftover Bolognese

This pasta bake is a good introduction to beef for your baby. A cheesy sauce often encourages them to try something new.

• •

Cook the pasta according to the package instructions, then drain.

Mix the Bolognese Sauce (see recipe opposite) and cooked pasta together and spoon the mixture into a baking dish. Preheat the broiler to high.

To make the cheese sauce, melt the butter in a saucepan. Add the flour and stir over the heat for a minute, then gradually add the milk, whisking continuously, until thickened. Remove from the heat, add the mustard and Parmesan, stir until the cheese has melted, then spoon the sauce on top of the pasta.

Place under the broiler for 10 minutes until bubbling.

Cottage Pie ❄

MAKES 4 CHILD PORTIONS
14 oz (400 g) white potatoes,
    peeled and diced
2 tablespoons milk
1–2 tablespoons butter
⅓ quantity Bolognese Sauce (see
    page 166), around 11 oz (300 g)
cooked peas and carrot stars,
    to serve (optional)

Leftover Bolognese

Cottage pie is the ultimate comfort food and the perfect winter warmer. Why not divide portions between individual dishes. Serving it like this is more appealing to children as they feel like they have their own very special dinner.

• •

Preheat the broiler to high. Put the potatoes in a saucepan of cold salted water, bring to a boil, then reduce the heat and simmer for about 15 minutes, until tender. Drain and mash with the milk and butter.

Divide the Bolognese Sauce (see page 166) between 4 small heatproof dishes and spoon the mashed potatoes on top.

Place under the hot broiler for 5–8 minutes until bubbling and golden on top. Remove, let cool slightly, and garnish with cooked peas and carrot stars.

Sweet Potato Boats

1 small sweet potato

3 tablespoons Bolognese Sauce

2 tablespoons grated aged
   Cheddar cheese

*Leftover
Bolognese*

An excellent source of vitamin A, sweet potato is packed full of goodness and acts as a fun and healthy "boat" for your bolognese. The quantities below can be doubled or tripled to serve a whole family.

Prick the sweet potato with a fork several times and microwave it for 7–10 minutes until soft in the middle, or bake in the oven at 400°F (200°C) for about 45 minutes, or until soft and cooked through.

Preheat the broiler to high. As soon as the potato is cool enough to handle, slice it in half vertically and scoop out some of the potato into a bowl. Mix it with the Bolognese Sauce (see page 166) and spoon it back into the "boat." Sprinkle with the cheese.

Place under a hot broiler for 5 minutes until the cheese has melted.

Serve with steamed broccoli florets.

Lamb Chops with Thyme, Garlic, and Lemon

DAIRY FREE

MAKES 4 CHILD PORTIONS
leaves from 4 sprigs fresh thyme
2 teaspoons lemon juice
1 garlic clove, crushed
2 tablespoons olive oil
4 lamb chops

These marinated lamb chops are beautifully tender. Cut into strips, the tender meat makes great finger food for young babies, or you can give them the chops whole, trimming off the fat and wrapping the bone to make it easier for them to hold.

● ●

Put the thyme sprigs in a bowl with the lemon juice, garlic, and oil. Add the lamb chops and coat them in the marinade. Marinate for at least 1 hour (ideally overnight).

Preheat the broiler to high. Put the marinated chops on a baking sheet or rack and broil about 8 in (20 cm) away from the broiler for 8–10 minutes, turning them halfway through the cooking time. This makes a "pink" medium-cooked chop. For a well-done chop, cook it under the broiler for 12–15 minutes.

Remove from the broiler, leave to rest for a few minutes, and serve with couscous (try my Cherub's Chicken Couscous, without the chicken, on page 125).

Swedish Meatballs ❄

MAKES 20 MEATBALLS
(4–5 CHILD PORTIONS)

Meatballs

11 oz (300 g) lean ground beef

⅓ cup dried breadcrumbs

⅓ cup finely grated
Parmesan cheese

1½ teaspoons chopped
fresh thyme

1 egg, beaten

a few dashes of Worcestershire
sauce

2–3 tablespoons canola
or sunflower oil

chopped fresh parsley to
garnish (optional)

Sauce

2 tablespoons sunflower oil

2 leeks, trimmed and finely sliced

1 garlic clove, crushed

1 cup unsalted or diluted
beef stock

⅞ cup sour cream

a few drops of Worcestershire
sauce

1 teaspoon balsamic vinegar

a little salt and pepper (for
babies over 12 months old)

Nothing beats homemade Swedish meatballs smothered in a creamy gravy sauce. This is a family favorite in my house.

• •

To make the meatballs, combine all the ingredients (except the oil and parsley) in a mixing bowl. Season with salt and pepper (if using), mix well, then shape the mixture into 20 equal-sized balls.

Heat the oil in a deep-sided skillet. Fry the meatballs (in batches if necessary) for 4–5 minutes, turning them occasionally, until golden on all sides but not completely cooked through. Set aside.

Now, make the sauce. Heat the oil in a saucepan, add the leeks, and cook gently over a low heat until they are completely soft. Add the garlic and fry for a few minutes, then add the stock. Simmer the sauce for 3–4 minutes until it has reduced by a third. Add the meatballs and simmer for 10 minutes more, until the meatballs are cooked through.

Stir in the sour cream, Worcestershire sauce, and vinegar, and heat through until bubbling, then serve with mashed potato (or my carrot and potato mash pie topping on page 145), sprinkling the meatballs with parsley if you wish.

Minty Lamb Koftas 🔵1+ year ❄

**MAKES 8 KOFTAS
(8 CHILD PORTIONS)**

1 tablespoon olive oil
1 small red onion, finely chopped
1 garlic clove, crushed
½ teaspoon ground cumin
8 oz (225 g) ground lamb
Scant 1/4 cup fresh breadcrumbs
2 teaspoons chopped
   fresh mint leaves
1 teaspoon honey
1 egg yolk
8 small pita breads, to serve
4 tablespoons Greek-style yogurt,
   to serve
sliced tomato and cucumber,
   to serve
a little salt and pepper

You will also need: 8 wooden
   skewers, soaked in warm
   water for 30 minutes

Children love to eat things on sticks, but these koftas are just as good stuffed into pitas or wraps (remove the skewer first), or you can use the ground lamb mixture to make burgers. Try them with a minty yogurt dressing.

• •

Heat the oil in a skillet, add the onion, and sauté for 5–6 minutes, until soft. Add the garlic and cumin, and cook for 1 minute more, then transfer to a bowl. Add the remaining ingredients (except the pita, yogurt, tomato, and cucumber), season with salt and pepper, and mix thoroughly. For a finer texture, process everything in the bowl of a food processor.

Divide the mixture into eight and form into balls. Thread a skewer through each ball and use your hand to firmly form each ball into a patty shape on the skewer. If you have time, chill the koftas on a plate in the refrigerator for 1–2 hours.

Preheat the broiler to high. Grill the koftas on a broiler rack for 8–10 minutes, turning halfway, until cooked through. Cool slightly before serving and remove the skewers for smaller children. Split the pitas and stuff a kofta into each one, along with some yogurt, tomato, and cucumber.

Tasty Beef Quesadillas

MAKES 12 WEDGES
(6 CHILD PORTIONS)
1 tablespoon sunflower oil
4 scallions, sliced
½ cup finely diced zucchini
½ sweet red bell pepper, seeded
  and finely diced
4¼ oz (110 g) lean ground beef
1 garlic clove, crushed
3 tablespoons drained
  canned sweet corn
1½ teaspoons mild curry paste
1 teaspoon sun-dried tomato paste
⅜ cup grated Cheddar cheese
4 small tortilla wraps

Children will love to help prepare their very own quesadilla creations.

• •

Heat the oil in a skillet, add the scallion, zucchini, and pepper, and sauté for 2 minutes.

Add the beef and fry with the vegetables until browned, breaking up any lumps of ground beef with a wooden spoon. Add the garlic, sweet corn, curry paste, and sun-dried tomato paste. Stir and simmer for 4 minutes.

Put a tortilla on a cutting board. Spoon half the mixture on top and spread to the edges. Sprinkle with half of the cheese. Top with another tortilla. Make a second quesadilla the same way,

Heat a large skillet until hot. Add a quesadilla and fry for 1 minute on each side, until golden, crisp, and the cheese has melted. Remove from the pan and repeat with the second quesadilla.

Remove from the heat and slice each quesadilla into 6 wedges. Serve with crudités and dips (see my dip recipes on pages 41).

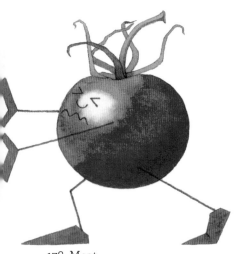

Steak with Roasted Vegetables

DAIRY FREE

MAKES 4 CHILD PORTIONS

½ teaspoon chopped fresh
rosemary leaves

1 tablespoon plus 1 teaspoon
light olive oil

11 oz (300 g) sirloin steak

Roasted Vegetables

6 oz (175 g) new potatoes, halved

1 small sweet potato, scrubbed
and cut into thin wedges
or fries

1 sweet yellow bell pepper, seeded
and cut into strips

½ sweet red bell pepper, seeded
and cut into strips

1 tablespoon olive oil

1 teaspoon finely chopped
rosemary leaves

1 teaspoon balsamic vinegar

6 button mushrooms,
halved if large

Red meat is good for young children because it provides the best source of iron. Serve with lots of sweet roasted veggie "fingers" for a nutritious mini adult meal.

● ●

Put the rosemary and 1 teaspoon of the light olive oil in a bowl, and add the steak, coating it in the aromatic oil.

Preheat the oven to 400°F (200°C). Put the potatoes (new and sweet) and bell peppers in a roasting pan. Add the oil and rosemary and roast for 20 minutes until golden. Add the balsamic vinegar and the mushrooms and roast for 10 minutes more.

Heat a skillet until hot, add the remaining light olive oil, and fry the steak for 2 minutes on each side. Remove from the pan and leave to rest for 5 minutes. Slice the steak into strips and serve with the roasted vegetables.

Mini Burgers ❄

MAKES 20 MINI BURGERS
1½ cups fresh breadcrumbs
1 small red onion, chopped
1 cup grated peeled carrot
½ cup grated peeled apple
9 oz (250 g) lean ground beef
1 small garlic clove, crushed
1 teaspoon chopped fresh thyme
¼ cup grated Parmesan cheese
mini slider burger rolls (optional)
carrot sticks, halved cherry
    tomatoes, and ketchup, to serve

Grated apple is the secret ingredient here. It makes the burgers succulent and tender, giving them a flavor that babies love. Simply process all the ingredients together in a blender and you're good to go. Freeze any leftover cooked burgers so you can prepare a home-cooked meal even on busy days.

• •

Place the breadcrumbs in the bowl of a food processor with the onion, carrot, apple, ground beef, garlic, thyme, and Parmesan, and process until finely chopped.

Transfer the burger mixture to a bowl and use your hands to shape it into 20 mini burgers.

Preheat the broiler to high. Line a baking sheet or rack with lightly greased foil.

Place the burgers on the baking sheet and place under the broiler for 5 minutes. Turn over and broil for 3–5 minutes more until lightly golden and cooked.

Serve in mini burger rolls, if you wish, with carrot sticks, cherry tomatoes, and ketchup.

Roast Beef

MAKES 5 ADULT PORTIONS
OR 10 CHILD PORTIONS

2 lb 2 oz (1 kg) topside
    roasting joint
1 tablespoon olive oil
fresh thyme leaves from 3 sprigs
a little salt and pepper (for
    babies over 12 months old)

Yorkshire Puddings
sunflower oil
1 cup all-purpose flour
3 eggs
⅔ cup whole milk

Gravy
2 tablespoons sunflower oil
2 tablespoons all-purpose flour
2 cups unsalted or diluted
    beef stock
½ teaspoon Worcestershire sauce
1 teaspoon tomato puree

Who doesn't love roast beef? This is the ultimate family Sunday meal. Cut the beef into strips for your baby's mouth, and serve it with a little gravy and some roasted vegetables like sweet potato and parsnips. The Yorkshire puddings are like large popovers, and are easy for your baby to hold onto and eat. I have also come up with two tasty recipes using leftover roast beef for your little one.

• •

Preheat the oven to 350°F (180°C).

Put the beef in a small roasting pan, drizzle with the oil, season with salt and pepper (if using), and scatter with thyme leaves. Roast for 50 minutes to 1 hour (for medium doneness), until golden and firm to the touch. Remove from the oven, cover with foil, and leave to rest for 20 minutes.

While the beef is resting, make the Yorkshire puddings. Increase the oven temperature to 400°F (200°C). Put a 12-hole deep muffin pan in the oven to get hot, then pour a thin layer of sunflower oil into each hole. Put the pan back into the oven for 5 minutes.

Place the flour in a bowl, make a well in the middle, add the eggs, then gradually pour in the milk, whisking continuously, until you have a smooth batter.

Ladle the batter into the 12 holes of the hot pan and put into the oven for 15–18 minutes until they've risen and are golden and crisp.

Place the beef on a cutting board. Pour the cooking juices into a mixing bowl. Add 2 tablespoons of oil to the pan the beef was roasted in and put the pan on the stovetop. Sprinkle in the flour and whisk over the heat for a few seconds before gradually whisking in the stock, until you have a thick and smooth mixture. Add the Worcestershire sauce, tomato puree, and some salt and pepper (if using), together with any beef cooking juices. Bring to a boil, then simmer, and reduce until you have a gravy consistency.

Carve the rested beef and serve it with the gravy and Yorkshire puddings, and green vegetables of your choice.

My First Beef Curry ❄

MAKES 4 CHILD PORTIONS

1 tablespoon sunflower oil

1 shallot, finely chopped

1 sweet red bell pepper,
   seeded and diced

2 garlic cloves, crushed

1 tablespoon mild curry paste

1 teaspoon garam masala

1¼ cups unsalted or
   diluted beef stock

1–2 teaspoons mango chutney

1 tablespoon apple juice

2 teaspoons cornstarch

¼ cup frozen peas

2–3 tablespoons heavy cream

⅞ cup diced leftover roast
   beef (approx. 4½ oz/120 g)

cooked basmati rice, to serve

Leftover Roast Beef

Here's a great recipe for introducing new tastes and textures to your little one. Babies are often open to accepting new tastes between the age of 6 and 12 months but can become more fussy toward the end of the first year, so take the opportunity to introduce lots of flavor combinations before their first birthday. The curry paste and garam masala here act as a tasty, subtle introduction to spices. You may find that your baby likes curry before he reaches his first birthday!

• •

Heat the oil in a wok or deep-sided skillet, add the shallot, bell pepper, and garlic, and stir-fry for 3 minutes, then add the curry paste and garam masala and fry for a few seconds.

Stir in the stock, mango chutney, and apple juice, bring to a boil, and simmer for 5 minutes. Mix the cornstarch with a little water and stir it into the curry sauce. Add the peas, cream, and diced beef, and stir until thickened and heated through. Serve with basmati rice.

Beef Croquettes

DAIRY FREE ✳

MAKES 12 CROQUETTES

9 oz (250 g) potatoes, peeled
   and diced
2 teaspoons olive oil
5 scallions, finely sliced
½ cup grated peeled carrot
1 cup chopped brown mushrooms
1 garlic clove, crushed
⅞ cup diced leftover roast beef
   (approx. 4½ oz/120 g)
2 teaspoons chopped fresh thyme
1 teaspoon tomato puree
2 teaspoons Worcestershire sauce
1 cup fresh breadcrumbs
a little all-purpose flour, for
   coating
2 tablespoons sunflower oil
a little salt and pepper (for babies
   over 12 months old)

Leftover Roast Beef

This is a great way to use up leftover roast beef. Little ones love to eat with their fingers and these beef croquettes are so easy to make. They're great for adults, too!

● ●

Put the potatoes in a saucepan of water, bring to a boil, and simmer for 10–12 minutes until soft. Drain, then mash until smooth. Leave to cool.

Heat the olive oil in a skillet, add the scallions, carrot, mushrooms, and garlic and fry over a high heat for 5 minutes until soft and any liquid from the mushrooms has evaporated. Remove from the heat and leave to cool.

Combine the cooled mashed potato, cold vegetables, diced beef, and the remaining ingredients (except the flour) in a mixing bowl and season lightly with salt and pepper (if using). Shape the mixture into 12 equal-sized croquettes. Place some flour on a plate and roll the croquettes in the flour.

Heat the sunflower oil in a skillet and fry the croquettes for 3–4 minutes (in 2 batches) until golden all over. Transfer to a plate lined with paper towels.

Sweet Things

Carrot and Banana Cookies

MAKES 15 COOKIES

1¼ cups chopped bananas
1 cup grated peeled carrots
⅔ cup raisins
2 heaping tablespoons smooth
 peanut butter
2 tablespoons sunflower oil
2–3 tablespoons agave syrup,
 maple syrup, or honey
½ teaspoon ground cinnamon
1 teaspoon mixed spice
1⅓ cups rolled oats

Here's a guilt-free sweet treat! Carrots, bananas, raisins, and oats make this a far healthier snack than most store-bought treats, as they don't contain refined sugar. Only use honey if serving to babies over 12 months old.

Preheat the oven to 350°F (180°C) and line a baking sheet with parchment paper.

Place the bananas in the bowl of a food processor and process until smooth. Add the remaining ingredients and pulse a few times to roughly combine.

Transfer the mixture to a bowl, then divide it into 15 equal-sized balls.

Place the balls on the lined baking sheet and, using wet hands, slightly flatten each ball. Bake in the oven for 20 minutes, or until light golden brown. Remove from the oven, let cool on the sheet for a few minutes, then transfer to a wire rack to cool completely.

Peanut Butter Cookies

MAKES 15 COOKIES

⅔ cup smooth peanut butter
½ cup ground almonds
⅓ cup golden raisins
½ cup dried unsweetened coconut
1 teaspoon vanilla extract
2 tablespoons maple syrup
a pinch of salt
2 tablespoons buckwheat flour
   or all-purpose flour
Heaped ⅛ cup chocolate chips
   (for dairy-free cookies, use
   dairy -free chocolate chips)

Babies are less likely to develop allergies if they are introduced to certain foods early on (see page 13). Peanut butter and finely ground nuts can be introduced from 6 months and these peanut butter cookies are a tasty way to introduce new flavors into your child's diet.

Preheat the oven to 325°F (160°C) and line two baking sheets with parchment paper.

Place all the ingredients, except the chocolate chips, in the bowl of a food processor and process until roughly chopped and the mixture has come together.

Transfer the cookie mixture to a mixing bowl and stir in the chocolate chips.

Shape the cookie dough into 15 equal-sized balls and place the balls on the lined sheets. Flatten them slightly and press the prongs of a fork gently onto each one. Bake for 12 minutes until lightly golden, then remove from the oven, let cool slightly on the sheets, then transfer to a wire rack to cool completely.

Zucchini, Orange, and Spice Muffins ❄

MAKES 18 MINI MUFFINS
OR 10 REGULAR MUFFINS
1⅓ cups self-rising flour
½ teaspoon baking powder
½ teaspoon baking soda
½ teaspoon pumpkin pie spice
a pinch of fine salt
½ cup freshly squeezed orange
   juice
grated zest of 1 medium orange
3 tablespoons butter, melted
1 egg
⅓ cup soft light brown sugar
1 zucchini, finely grated
   (approx. 1 cup)
⅓ cup golden raisins

Tip

★ To reheat frozen muffins, remove them from the freezer container and leave to defrost at room temperature overnight. Alternatively, reheat from frozen in the oven at 350°F (180°C) for 10–15 minutes (or for less time if reheating mini muffins).

Here's a tasty way to eat your greens! These deliciously moist muffins are low in sugar, too, and you can make them as mini versions or regular sized. Either way, they freeze well, so are an excellent snack to have on hand.

• •

Preheat the oven to 350°F (180°C) and line two 12-hole mini muffin pans with 18 mini muffin paper liners, or one regular 12-hole muffin pan with 10 paper liners.

Sift the flour, baking powder, baking soda, pumpkin pie spice, and salt into a large bowl and stir to combine.

Whisk the orange juice, zest, melted butter, egg, and sugar together in a mixing bowl until well combined.

Stir the wet ingredients into the dry ingredients, then fold in the grated zucchini and golden raisins. Spoon the mixture into the muffin liners and bake for 12–15 minutes for mini muffins or 22–25 minutes for regular muffins, until a wooden skewer inserted into one of the muffins comes out clean.

Remove from the oven and let cool on a wire rack.

Spiced Apple and Date Squares

MAKES 20 SQUARES

2¼ cups rolled oats
½ cup dried unsweetened coconut
⅜ cup finely chopped pecans
½ cup roughly chopped pitted dates
⅔ cup boiling water
½ cup sunflower oil
1 teaspoon vanilla extract
⅓ cup honey
1 teaspoon ground cinnamon
¼ teaspoon pumpkin pie spice
½ cup finely chopped dried apple

Dried fruit is a good source of fiber, iron, and energy. Adding a little pumpkin pie spice to these snacks will add interest to the cakes and pairing the spice and oats with apple, date, and coconut transforms this healthy bake into an irresistible treat.

• •

Preheat the oven to 400°F (200°C) and line a 8 in (20 cm) square cake pan with plastic wrap.

Combine the oats, coconut, and pecans in a bowl, then spread them out on a baking sheet. Bake for 10–15 minutes, stirring halfway through, until lightly toasted. Remove from the oven and let cool.

Put the dates and boiling water in the bowl of a small blender or processor and blend until smooth.

Place the oil, vanilla, honey, and date mixture in a saucepan and heat until dissolved. Remove from the heat, add the toasted oat mixture, spices, and apple, and stir until combined.

Spoon the mixture into the cake pan and level the surface. Refrigerate for 2 hours before inverting onto a plate. Remove the plastic wrap, and cut into 20 squares. Store in an airtight container for 2–3 days.

Strawberry and Rhubarb Crumble

MAKES 6 CHILD PORTIONS

¼ cup ground almonds

14 oz (400 g) trimmed rhubarb, cut into ¾ in (2 cm) lengths

⅔ cup hulled and halved fresh strawberries

4 tablespoons superfine sugar

Crumble

1¼ cups all-purpose flour

a generous pinch of fine salt

½ cup cubed cold butter

⅓ cup light brown sugar

½ cup ground almonds

A good crumble is comfort food at its best, and I love the combination of rhubarb and strawberries. Sprinkle ground almonds over the base of the dish to soak up some of the juices from the fruit, so that they don't bubble up over the top when it's cooking.

• •

Preheat the oven to 400°F (200°C).

To make the topping, mix the flour with the salt in a bowl and work in the butter using your fingertips until the mixture resembles breadcrumbs, then stir in the light brown sugar and ground almonds. Alternatively, place the ingredients in a food processor and process briefly.

Sprinkle the ground almonds over the base of an ovenproof dish (about 7 in / 17 cm in diameter). Mix the rhubarb and strawberries with the sugar and pour into the dish.

Cover the fruit with the crumble topping and sprinkle over a tablespoon of water (this will help to make the topping crispy). Bake for about 25 minutes, until the crumble topping is golden brown.

Remove from the oven and allow to cool slightly before serving.

Carrot, Maple, and Golden Raisin Muffins

MAKES 24 MINI MUFFINS

2 eggs
½ cup unsalted butter, softened
⅓ cup soft dark brown sugar
2 tablespoons maple syrup
1 teaspoon pumpkin pie spice
1 teaspoon baking powder
⅞ cup self-rising flour
½ cup grated peeled carrot
⅓ cup golden raisins
4½ tablespoons cream cheese
24 fresh raspberries
confectioners' sugar, to dust

Carrot works so well in muffins, keeping the mixture moist and delicious, and mini versions are the perfect size for busy little fingers.

•••

Preheat the oven to 325°F (160°C) and line a 24-hole mini-muffin pan with mini-muffin liners.

Place all the ingredients (except the cream cheese, raspberries, and confectioners' sugar) in a mixing bowl and whisk with an electric hand-held whisk. Alternatively, use a stand mixer.

Divide the mixture evenly between the paper liners and bake for 18 minutes, or until well risen and lightly golden. Remove from the oven and let cool on a wire rack.

To serve, spread each cooled muffin with a teaspoon of cream cheese, garnish with a raspberry, and dust with confectioners' sugar.

Mini Energy Balls

DAIRY FREE

MAKES 30 BALLS

1⅛ cup pitted dates

3 tablespoons smooth
   peanut butter

3 tablespoons sunflower oil

⅜ cup dried unsweetened coconut

3 tablespoons sunflower seeds

1⅓ cups oz rolled oats

¼ cup raisins

⅛ cup very finely chopped pecans

1 tablespoon chia seeds

¾ cup crispy rice cereal

a pinch of salt (for babies
   over 12 months old)

**Try these delicious healthy snacks to give you or
your child a mid-morning or afternoon energy boost.**

• •

Put the dates in a saucepan with ½ cup boiling water.
Cover with a lid, bring to a boil, and simmer for 2
minutes. Remove from the heat and set aside for 5
minutes.

Transfer the soaked date mixture to a blender or food
processor and process until smooth (or blend in a
bowl using a hand-held electric blender).

Place the peanut butter and date mixture in a saucepan
and melt over a low heat until smooth. Remove from
the heat and add the remaining ingredients to the
saucepan. Stir well to combine, then shape into 30
equal-sized little balls. Place the balls on a plate and
refrigerate for 1 hour before eating.

Store in the refrigerator in an airtight container, for up
to 5 days.

Strawberry Rice Pudding

MAKES 6 CHILD PORTIONS
¼ cup short-grain round white
   rice, such as arborio
2¾ cup whole milk
¼ teaspoon vanilla extract
2 tablespoons unsalted butter,
   plus extra for greasing
sugar-free strawberry jam,
   to serve

This is a quick and tasty way to cook rice pudding, and kids love it. Stir in some strawberry jam for an added fruity flavor (use sugar-free strawberry jam for babies under one).

Preheat the oven to 300°F (150°C) and grease an ovenproof dish with butter.

Place the rice, milk, and vanilla extract in the dish and stir well. Dot the surface with butter then bake the pudding for 30 minutes. Remove from the oven and stir, then continue to bake for 1–1½ hours until the rice is cooked. Remove the dish from the oven, let it cool slightly, and serve each portion topped with a little sugar-free strawberry jam.

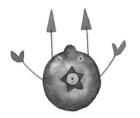

Crispy Rice, Oat, and Peanut Butter Bars

MAKES 12 BARS
¼ cup soft light brown sugar
⅔ cup smooth peanut butter
⅓ cup maple syrup
⅓ cup unsalted butter, softened
2 cups crispy rice cereal
½ cup rolled oats
½ cup chopped pecans
⅓ cup golden raisins
⅓ cup finely chopped dried
   apricots

This is a peanut butter-lover's dream treat. It's delicious and so simple to make with budding little chefs.

• •

Line a 8 in (20cm) square baking dish with plastic wrap, letting it overhand the sides.

Measure the cereal, oats, pecans, golden raisins, and apricots into a food processor. Pulse three times very quickly to roughly chop the ingredients.

Place the sugar, peanut butter, maple syrup, and butter in a saucepan and gently warm over a low heat until the mixture is dissolved and smooth.

Remove the saucepan from the heat and add the dry ingredients. Mix well, then spoon into the square baking dish. Level the top, cover, and refrigerate for 3–4 hours until completely firm.

When firm, invert onto a plate, remove the plastic wrap and cut into 12 bars. Store the bars in an airtight container in the refrigerator for 4–5 days.

Carrot, Coconut, and Raisin Bites

DAIRY FREE

½ cup pitted dates
½ cup boiling water
½ cup pecans
½ cup dried unsweetened coconut
1 cup grated peeled carrots
½ teaspoon pumpkin pie spice
3 tablespoons raisins
2 tablespoons sunflower oil
½ cup rolled oats
a good pinch of salt (for
   babies over 12 months old)

These make the perfect healthy snack for little ones. They contain no refined sugar and the natural sweetness comes from the dates, carrots, and raisins.

Put the dates in a saucepan with the boiling water. Cover with a lid, bring to a boil, and simmer for 2 minutes. Remove from the heat and set aside for 5 minutes.

Put the pecans in a food processor and process until finely chopped, then set aside.

Put the soaked dates and 2 tablespoons of the soaking liquid in a food processor. Process until smooth, then add the remaining ingredients, including the chopped pecans. Process again briefly, until the mixture has come together but is still coarse.

Shape the mixture into 20 balls, place the balls on a plate, and refrigerate for at least 1 hour before eating. The balls will keep in the refrigerator for up to 2 days.

Summer Fruit Yogurt Ice Cream

MAKES 6 CHILD PORTIONS

11 oz (300 g) mixed frozen
   berries, such as raspberries,
   blackberries, and blueberries,
   thawed at room temperature or
   heated gently in a saucepan or
   microwave
7 fl oz (200 ml) heavy cream
1⅔ cup plain yogurt
⅓ cup superfine sugar

Making frozen yogurt is easier than you might think —it can be made without an ice-cream maker.

• •

Puree and sieve half the summer fruits to remove the seeds.

Lightly whisk the cream in a bowl until it forms soft peaks. Fold together with the yogurt, cream, superfine sugar (reserving one tablespoon), and the fruit puree.

Freeze in an ice-cream machine, following the manufacturer's instructions. When frozen but still with a soft texture, mix the remaining summer fruits with the remaining tablespoon of superfine sugar and stir them into the ice-cream mixture.

Alternatively, spoon the ice-cream mixture into a freezer container and place in the freezer. When half frozen, remove and beat well until smooth and ice crystals are broken down, either using an electric hand-held whisk or in a food processor. Mix the rest of the fruit with the tablespoon of superfine sugar and stir it into the yogurt ice cream. Return to the freezer and stir one or two more times during the freezing process to get a smooth ice cream.

Chocolate Beet Brownies

MAKES 25 SQUARES

7 oz (200 g) dark chocolate, chopped

½ cup cubed unsalted butter

3 large eggs

1 teaspoon vanilla extract

1 cup superfine sugar

¾ cup self-rising flour

¼ cup cocoa powder

1½ cups (300 g/11 oz) grated cooked beets

confectioner's sugar, for dusting (optional)

These brownies are chocolate heaven, and what a great way to boost your 5-a-day!

Preheat the oven to 325°F (160°C) and line an 8 in (20 cm) square cake pan with parchment paper.

Melt the chocolate and butter together in a large heatproof bowl over a saucepan of simmering water.

When completely melted, remove the bowl, let cool slightly, then add the eggs, vanilla extract, and sugar, and whisk using an electric hand-held whisk until combined. Then add the flour, cocoa powder, and beets. Whisk again, then spoon the mixture into the cake pan. Bake for 30 minutes until the cake is set and just firm in the middle. Remove from the oven and let cool. Remove from the cake pan and cut into 25 squares. Dust with confectioner's sugar, if wished. Store in an airtight container in the refrigerator, or at room temperature, for up to 2 days.

Peach, Apple, and Berry Crumble ❄

MAKES 6 CHILD PORTIONS

2 tablespoons butter

2 Pink Lady apples (or other sweet eating apple), peeled, cored, and diced

2 ripe peaches, skinned, pitted, and diced

4 tablespoons soft light brown sugar

1 cup fresh blueberries

1¼ cups fresh raspberries

Crumble

1 cup all-purpose flour

¼ cup rolled oats

⅓ cup cubed cold butter

4 tablespoons soft light brown sugar

This light crumble is bursting with a gooey peach, berry, and apple filling. It's full of antioxidants from the berries and fiber from the peach and apple, and it is an easy way to get your child eating and enjoying more fruit.

• •

Preheat the oven to 350°F (180°C).

To make the fruit filling, melt the butter in a saucepan. Add the diced apple and peach and sauté for 3 minutes, then stir in the sugar. Remove from the heat, stir in the berries, and spoon the mixture into an 8 in (20 cm) ovenproof dish or 6 individual ovenproof pots.

Mix all of the crumble topping ingredients together in a bowl. Work in the butter using your fingertips until the mixture resembles coarse breadcrumbs. Alternatively, place the ingredients in a food processor and process briefly.

Scatter the topping over the fruit and bake until bubbling and golden on top (25–30 minutes if using a large dish, 20 minutes for the pots).

Remove from the oven and allow to cool slightly before serving.

Egg- and Dairy-free Chocolate Cake

MAKES 10 CHILD PORTIONS

Chocolate Cake
¾ cup sunflower oil
¼ cup golden syrup, such as
  Lyle's, alternatively substitute
  light corn syrup
2 teaspoons vanilla extract
2 cups boiling water
⅔ cup cocoa powder
3⅔ cups self-rising flour
1 cup superfine sugar
1 teaspoon baking powder
2 teaspoons baking soda

Chocolate Frosting and Filling
⅓ cup dairy-free margarine
⅓ cup soy cream cheese, such as
  Tofutti
1¼ cups confectioners' sugar,
  plus extra to dust
½ cup cocoa powder
1 teaspoon vanilla extract
¾ cup chopped dairy-free
  chocolate, plus extra to
  grate and decorate
8 tablespoons seedless
  raspberry jam, warmed

Just because you have an allergy doesn't mean you can't enjoy a good cake. This crowd-pleaser is great for children's parties.

• •

Preheat the oven to 325°F (160°C) and grease and line the bases of 2 x 8 in (20 cm) round cake pans.

Stir the oil, syrup, vanilla, and boiling water together in a large bowl until well combined. Sift in the cocoa powder and flour, then add the sugar, baking powder, and baking soda, and whisk until light and fluffy. Divide the mixture between the two pans. Bake for 30–35 minutes until risen and firm in the middle. Remove from the oven and transfer to a wire rack to cool.

For the frosting, whisk the margarine, cream cheese, and confectioners' sugar together in a bowl until light and fluffy. Stir in the cocoa powder and vanilla extract. Melt the chocolate in a heatproof bowl over a saucepan of simmering water, then let cool before adding it to the bowl. Whisk until it thickens.

Put one of the cakes on a cake stand. Brush half the warm jam over the top. Spread a third of the frosting on top, right to the edges. Place the second cake on top and brush with the remaining jam. Frost the top and sides with the remaining frosting. Decorate with grated chocolate and dust with confectioners' sugar.

INDEX

The must-have recipe app

Moms everywhere rely on Annabel's award-winning Baby & Toddler Recipe App. Filled with more than 250 delicious, nutritious recipes, simple planners, shopping lists, and more, it's the handiest of guides for easy mealtime inspiration – whether you're cooking for baby, toddler or the whole family.

Available on iPhone and Android.

Be a part of the AK Club

Join the AK Club for free today and discover exclusive recipes and special content, insider news, competitions, plus a host of great offers. You can also be a part of Annabel's world on social media too.

www.annabelkarmel.com

annabelkarmel   annabelkarmel   annabelkarmel

Thanks to:

Sarah Louise Smith, Lucinda McCord, Dave King, Emma Smith, Laura Nickoll, Sarah Almond Bushell MPhill, BSc RD, Dr Adam Fox MA, Nadine Wickenden, Jonathan Lloyd, Tamsin Weston, Maud Eden, Kostas Stavrinos, Lucy Staley, Lara Karmel, Chloe Leeser, Marina Magpoc, Ebury.

A special thank you to our cover-star finalists: Darcy Beresford, Harlen Bodhi White, Evie Lilly Gallacher, Milan McIntyre, and Lola Sokeyo.

www.stmartins.com

Photography by Dave King
Designed by Smith & Gilmour, London
Project management by Laura Nickoll

Library of Congress Cataloging-in-Publication Data

Names: Karmel, Annabel, author.
Title: Baby-led weaning recipe book : 120 recipes to let your baby take the lead / Annabel Karmel.
Description: First U.S. edition. | New York : St. Martin's Griffin, 2019. | Includes index.
Identifiers: LCCN 2018047941| ISBN 97812 50201362 (hardcover) | ISBN 9781250201379 (ebook)
Subjects: LCSH: Infants—Weaning. | Baby foods. | LCGFT: Cookbooks.
Classification: LCC RJ216 .K362 2019 | DDC 641.5/6222—dc23
LC record available at https://lccn.loc.gov/2018047941

Our books may be purchased in bulk for promotional, educational, or business use. Please contact your local bookseller or the Macmillan Corporate and Premium Sales Department at 1-800-221-7945, extension 5442, or by email at MacmillanSpecialMarkets@macmillan.com.

First published in Great Britain by Annabel Karmel

First U.S. Edition: April 2019

10 9 8 7 6 5 4 3 2 1